I0840741

CONTEMPORARY CONDITIONS OF HATE & MORAL LAW
VS
CHRISTIANS AND HOLY SCRIPTURE

INVESTIGATING HOW THINGS SEEM AND THE TRUTH

Jimmy Bricker, D.Div; PhD

authorHOUSE®

AuthorHouse™
1663 Liberty Drive
Bloomington, IN 47403
www.authorhouse.com
Phone: 1 (800) 839-8640

© 2019 Jimmy Bricker, D.Div; PhD. All rights reserved.

No part of this book may be reproduced, stored in a retrieval system, or transmitted by any means without the written permission of the author.

Scripture taken from The Holy Bible, King James Version. Public Domain

Scripture quotations are from the ESV® Bible (The Holy Bible, English Standard Version®), copyright © 2001 by Crossway, a publishing ministry of Good News Publishers. Used by permission. All rights reserved

Common English Bible (CEB)
Copyright © 2011 by Common English Bible

Published by AuthorHouse 05/03/2019

ISBN: 978-1-7283-1074-9 (sc)
ISBN: 978-1-7283-1073-2 (e)

Library of Congress Control Number: 2019906268

Print information available on the last page.

Any people depicted in stock imagery provided by Getty Images are models, and such images are being used for illustrative purposes only.
Certain stock imagery © Getty Images.

This book is printed on acid-free paper.

Because of the dynamic nature of the Internet, any web addresses or links contained in this book may have changed since publication and may no longer be valid. The views expressed in this work are solely those of the author and do not necessarily reflect the views of the publisher, and the publisher hereby disclaims any responsibility for them.

CONTENTS

ABSTRACT

The background for this book lies with the proliferation of attacks on Christianity by a progressive cultural movement. Christians are asking how to respond. Every day there is a bombardment of news that tends to inaccurately use Christianity against Christians. Franklin Graham spoke of this movement in an article titled "When Truth is Labeled 'Hate Speech' (Graham, 2019). Dr. Alex McFarland also equated these current events to the abandonment of moral law. He made the following quote in his recent newsletter: *"In the Classroom, Through Media, in Entertainment and via Rigidly Enforced Corporate Policies, Accommodation of Clear Moral Truth Is Being Squelched with Unrelenting Pressure"* (McFarland, 2019).

Additionally, we read where longtime stable denominations are easing back on interpretations of the inerrant and infallible Word to accommodate the cultural onslaught being levied at them. J. D. Greear, President of the Southern Baptist Convention stated in a podcast that being Christian is being privileged. Not in the sense that serving God is a privilege but that as a Christian we receive certain privileges in society that a non-Christian may not experience (Klett, 2019). Greear was quickly criticized for abandoning the inerrant Word by attempting to make the gospel relevant to today's culture whereas *"Paul said 'I am what I am by the grace of God – be ye reconciled through Christ.'"* A clear statement that we should reconcile with the teachings of the Bible and not It to us. In looking into the subject of how privilege is being applied to so many things, I found no end to how many ways the word is used in the context of being hateful. A couple of titles follow: "Don't Believe in Christian Privilege? These 15 Examples Will Leave No Doubt" (Johnson, 2016) and "30+ Examples of Christian Privilege" (Killermann, 2012). The dates of these titles reveal that the discussion of "Christian" and "privilege" date well before comments from the Southern Baptist Convention of 2019.

The issues confronting Christianity are plentiful. Only a unified voice of pragmatic and truthful rebuttal from the Christian community can these affronts be countered.

PURPOSE

This book seeks to catalog the extent of the cultural movement to appropriate Christianity today by molding the Word to fit the culture. A second objective is to provide counter arguments to the movement suggesting believers need to be relevant to the infallible Word instead. My position is that only through a unified voice speaking the truth of the Word can Christianity maintain its rightful religious prominence in this country. Highlighting of current Christian issues and Christian responses will add to the repertoire of knowledge for further research on this subject.

BACKGROUND

It is seen almost every day that scripture is being used to serve the moment. Politicians use bits and pieces of scripture to fit their narrative often completely out of context to scriptures before and after their quote. Noticeably, their use of scripture seems more like an attempt to throw the beliefs of Christians as a counterpunch to the values of Christians as in creating a circular fallacy using one's own words.

Speaking an untruth often enough without rebuttal creates a doubt in the minds of those listening. Objective accomplished they say. There appears to be an increase in the attempts to use Biblical passages and commandments to demonstrate hate. Virtually everything that one says today can be twisted into being hate speech at or about something. Accompanying these viral assaults is the new trend of changing the definition of words to suit the cause.

Christians wonder what is going on and how do we react and respond. Bringing together a current presentation of the many attempts where parts of our culture are using Christianity against Christians partnered with rebuttals and wisdom from both past and contemporary recognized Christian leaders will provide additional knowledge to the inventory of material on this subject. The Bible addresses today's issue in suitable fashion. The strategies of today are not new. Controlled immigration is not turning your backs on the poor. Believing in man and woman in marriage is not a hateful position to hold. When did walls become the focus of morality and is this a new definition?

METHODS

The approach taken must focus on clarity. This is best done organizing the chapters as point-counter point. The title of this book can be endlessly lengthy given the abundance of instances insinuated in the title. Be it from discussing privilege to hate speech, the pool of situations that can be researched in literature and the media is abundant. What is less abundant if not sparse is a focused effort to confront the verbal assault on Christianity using moral law and the inerrant and infallible Word of God. In many cases, religious denominations seem to be backing down in front of the assault.

I think that the timing is correct to add to the discussion a current composite of the issue to one spot. Future researchers on this matter will not have to search out the bits of information and perhaps an outcome will be that by collecting the counter arguments of Biblical statements and theologists' wisdom Christians will have some inerrant and infallible rebuttals to this component of cultural movement.

CONSTRAINTS

Discussions on cultural movements and Christianity date from the early days of New Testament writings. Many instances predate the New Testament. These movements are not new, nor will they be ceasing anytime soon. It would be unwise to think that anything more than a moment in time can be captured on this subject in one undertaking. With this constraint in mind, it is hoped that what is chronicled in my book can at least highlight the issue and be useful for further research.

TENTATIVE CHAPTER ARRANGEMENT BASED ON ISSUE:

1. Introduction
2. Climate Change and the Word
3. Abortion and the Word
4. Religion & Politics and the Word
5. Your Vocation and the Word
6. Social Justice and Christianity
7. The Cultural Church
8. Value Judging and the Word
9. Pride and Spiritual Struggles
10. Persecution
11. Intercessory Prayer, Praying for God to Intercede

INTRODUCTION

The chapters that follow are framed around a phenomenological and ethnographic look at the Contemporary Conditions of Hate and Moral Law vs Christians and Holy Scripture. Phenomenology is coupled with ethnography in this paper. The reason is that culture shifting is pervasive in the debates. From this perspective it can be observed that both behaviors and constraints are in active play. Evading the academic study of phenomenology, "lifeworld", "intersubjectivity", and "neoma" can be seen in today's happenings. These represent "causes" for positions. From an ethnographic view, the story of the cultural shift is still unfolding, and the shifts are developing greater divides. These chapters are written as a record of events of the day and which Biblical message is involved. It is not a record of a specific qualitative research methodology but is documentation better known as sermon material.

The depiction of the issues discussed in this paper is not an "us" and "them" picture. Christians turn on Christians as well for many of the reason's others have turned on Christians. It is all in how you interpret Scripture and how extensive have you studied the context of those Scriptures with their related mentions in other books of the Bible. An example is the deluge of negative comments received by pastor Dave Adamson from his Christian blog audience over one of his blogs. His comments about that experience can be found in his blog titled "Dave Adamson: The price of Christian free speech". (Adamson, 2019).

The material for these chapters has been endless since the 2016 election of the current Federal administration. Part of what has given rise to the vocal and persistent rise of nothing less than hate for Christian values by several outspoken bodies was the voter support the current administration apparently got by evangelical Christians. This may or may not be accurately depicted by the polls though the characterization seems there to stay. Of course, Christian doctrines state several of today's trends are not Biblical. Homosexuality is naturally a lightning rod for Biblical followers as is abortion. It doesn't end there. It goes deeper and over time has gotten more personal for Christians.

The treatment of migrants is a hotly contested Biblical interpretation issue. Bible verses are being used by both sides of this debate in an attempt to add credence to their arguments. An entire chapter is devoted to the mischaracterization of Bible verses that shows the multitude of debating fallacies used. There are nuances in the protests against Christian values that boil over into a person's vocation, climate change opinion, judging of issues, political preference, and of course abortion stance. Social justice is an evolutionary term. Definitions of words and terms change depending on which group of people use the word. Justice is a strongly held Biblical principle. Social justice does not have a legitimate definition for many as it is not Biblical justice and is again misrepresented and used against Christians. Again, this is an issue where Biblical verses are used by both sides of the argument. Churches and denominations are now discussing the culture of the church. Some have become more liberalized to satisfy their congregations and others have, against resistance, maintained their original doctrines. These discussions have been ongoing in 2019 and the final story is yet unfolding. This has led to Christians evaluating their own spirituality in light of the abundance of questioning opinions they confront.

In researching the abundance of real time phenomena's, the subject of "pride" became inescapable. What is leading to such hard and fast positions and how is it that it is so difficult to find any middle ground on these differences?

Studying the phenomena is incomplete without examining the effect the occurrence is having. Each chapter attempts to explore some of the ethnographic ramifications of what is happening. The debates appear to be creating cultural divides. On the surface, some of these divides have already expanded to the point that reconciliation may be impossible. The identifiers such as "I'm an American" or "I'm a Christian" may not be easily understood as identification of a neatly defined culture.

The abortion debate is the framework of a chapter. The cultural divide of the nation is evident by which states are liberalizing abortion and which states are passing more conservative legislation. Christian values are also being used by both sides of the climate change debate. Forget science and the money that finances the science. Depending on how you interpret certain Bible passages, you are likely to hold one opinion over another. The truth here is that cherry picking your passages will give you an entirely different conclusion depending on the passages read. The debate has led to some very entertaining observations. It was collecting the material for the chapter on climate change that triggered the thought that an entire paper should be focused on "what is the truth". Any part of the Bible could be cited, and a simple statement could be made about it as "being the truth" provided that the depth of passage research included both the Old Testament and the New Testament and other books of the Bible where the same subject is discussed. Each Biblical subject reviewed would invariably be applicable to some discussion that is happening in today's environment. The Bible is inerrant, written with clarity, provides us with what we need to know (necessity) and has sufficiency for our needs.

Considerable information can be ascertained by merely observing the lack of accepting the truth as being the truth. Bobby Jamieson drew this conclusion in "A Deeper Look at What the Bible Says about Truth". "Philosopher Roger Scruton has argued, "All discourse and dialogue depend upon the concept of truth. To agree with another is to accept the truth of what he says; to disagree is to reject it."[1] In other words, we can't even talk to each other without the notion of truth. To say that I'm lying is to presuppose there is truth to be told. To say that I'm wrong or even mistaken assumes the existence of a truth from which my statement departs." (Jamieson, 2019).

The chapters have avoided using the term "atheist" or other like term to define the anti-Christian movement. There is this exert from the American Thinker by E. M. Cadwaladr that perhaps provides sufficient linkage between atheism and politics to set the stage for a background thought while reading the chapters. It reads: "Uninterested in hard materialism, today's atheists believe in an emotional narrative invented and reinvented at the whim of politically motivated human beings. Today's atheism is not a philosophical position, but a political one. Superficially, the anti-Christian movement espouses the view that Christianity is *uniquely* evil in its intolerance – their word for the fact that we have standards. Christianity, like Western civilization, is squeezed into the usual Marxist mold as just another instrument of oppression. But without batting an eye, many of today's atheists manage to believe that Islam, an objectively more intolerant, more misogynistic, and far more bloodthirsty system of beliefs than Christianity – is somehow forgivable, or even a net social boon. In truth, the new atheism isn't about helping the "oppressed" – any more than it is about the non-belief in God or the exclusive belief in the world we can grasp with our senses. It is about being a vocal part of the identity group of avid Christian-haters. A political entity. It is about inventing yet another substitute sense of identity and purpose to replace the Christian sense of identity and purpose that it struggles to destroy." (Cadwaladr, 2018). The entirety of this article is worth reading.

There is also this challenging view about liberalism and the anti-Christian movement by Andrew Sullivan: "And this is how they threaten liberal democracy. They do not believe in the primacy of the individual, they believe the ends justify the means, they do not allow for doubt or reason, and their religious politics can brook no compromise. They demonstrate, to my mind, how profoundly liberal democracy has actually depended on the complement of a tolerant Christianity to sustain itself — as many earlier liberals (Tocqueville, for example) understood."

"It is Christianity that came to champion the individual conscience against the collective, which paved the way for individual rights. It is in Christianity that the seeds of Western religious toleration were first sown. Christianity is the only monotheism that seeks no sway over Caesar, that is content with the ultimate truth over the immediate satisfaction of power. It was Christianity that gave us successive social movements, which enabled more people to be included in the liberal project, thus renewing it. It was on these foundations that liberalism was built, and it is by these foundations it has endured. The question we face in contemporary times is whether a political system built upon such a religion can endure when belief in that religion has become a shadow of its future self." (Sullivan, 2018). Sullivan makes these comments by earlier by suggesting liberalism, socialism and anti-Christian movements have turned into a religion of their own, absent Christ.

Absent Christ

Romans 8:6 says, "For to be selfishly minded is death; but to be spiritually minded is life and peace".

The culture of today is the result of treating symptoms rather than treating the source of all of the discourse. Opioid epidemic, full prison system, school shootings and campus uproars are the telling signs that something in our societal psyche is not congruent. Behavior generally has a cause or ignition stimuli. People are becoming focused on themselves and though they talk about equality for all, they really mean equality for me. This internal focus looks for euphoria in the real, tangible world. First, that world does not provide the completeness that the souls we were born with is yearning to obtain. The spirit is not complete with only what the tangible world can provide. The inner person has to be satisfied as well. Jeremiah 17:9 describes the deceitfulness of the heart. A fallen world and sin are the source of unrest and angry discourse being witnessed in society today.

The United States was organized around Biblical principles. Many people had input as to how this country's government would be developed. Even though our major governing documents show a strong adherence to Biblical principles, not all of the minds that input into the government's organization were necessarily Christian. Though perhaps several were not Protestant Christians, they had a respect for the principles espoused in the

Bible. They had an internal acceptance of the guidance the Bible put forth that they agreeably felt that these principles should be the foundation of this country's government. They understood the truth in the Bible and therefore framed our Constitution on Biblical principles.

Returning to the trend towards being self-centered, the fabric of behavior that used be the education within the family weakened over the decades. What was expected to be educational foundations provided within the family unit are severely missing today. The family unit provided the format for social behavior, neighborly love and respect for others. As the family unit began to renege on its traditional job, the general population began to feel the consequences.

A part of the family responsibility had been religious guidance. It was from this education that the moral principles were introduced and taught. The family unit also made sure that their values were taught in the schools that they children attended. Local school boards were part of our founding establishment for the sole reason to ensure that the school mirrored the values of the community in its teaching. Obviously, the local community has lost considerable influence over the education of their children over time and the results are showing. The upcoming generations are leaving the school system with only part of the story being told and the part they have is devoid of instruction on their responsibility for the greater good of society.

Church denominations also modernized and softened their message to be more acceptable with the new community. The evangelical movement tries to keep true to the truth of the Bible and offered an alternative to the traditional denomination church. Though good for theology, it fractured the unified voice that denominations once had in terms of influencing the political environment in America. With this gap in the moral education, other philosophies were able to establish eventually leading to the idea that mankind is supreme and master of their own world. Denying that we are the product of a supreme Creator and are in a world that that Creator controls amplified the concept that man can do it all alone. Christians understand the subtleness of God's hand in managing our lives and our world. The Fall is real, and our world is the result of the Fall. Satisfying that inner longing of the soul can only be met by accepting Jesus as our Savior and trying best we can to live by the principles of the Bible fully understanding that we need to interpret the message as presented in its entirety and not by verse to verse.

As these chapters are read be guided by Mark 12:29-31: "And Jesus answered him, the first of all the commandments is, Hear, O Israel; The Lord our God is one Lord: and thou shalt love the Lord thy God with all thy heart, and with all thy soul, and with all thy mind, and with all thy strength: this is the first commandment. And the second is like, namely this, Thou shalt love they neighbor as thyself."

CLIMATE CHANGE AND THE WORD

Christian Faith and Climate Change

Christianity has been entangled into many political and scientific debates over the years. The current discussions regarding climate change appear to be using Christians as a form of leverage to support an environmental cause. Daily Christian groups and denominations are either defending their Biblical position or compromising their positions to appear modern and accepting. Even the Catholic Church has created an entire body to produce a church wide position on the subject. Several evangelical groups have constructed committees and task forces to render position papers.

This chapter presents several topics that are frequently advanced by both advocates and theologians. For as many that see a Biblical and Christian connection to our human impact on climate, there is an equal number that adhere to a contrary interpretation of the Bible and Christian stewardship.

The first topic is human over population and its impact on the planet. The first review covers the "go forth and multiply" command in Genesis. Scientific debate also enters the equation as does how we have coped historically with a growing population.

A strong effort is exerted by all sides of the debate on what being a good steward is and how the Bible plays into the various discussions on stewardship responsibilities. The stewardship factor is a centerpiece in the debate in almost all the positions. Different interpretations of Biblical application seem to be the dividing line between the different factions.

History has been a good educator on human adaptability. The section that addresses how it is that we still survive having created the calamity on earth that we humans have leans on the faith Christians have in the Word. The section following gets at the core of the continued doomsday philosophy that is so prevalent in the discussion on climate change and human impact. Here it is presented that if persuasion doesn't work, try scaring people into your court. Some of the strongest challenges for Christian in this discussion arise from the bombardment of media efforts applying guilt. As can be expected, some of the strongest pushback by Christians is against the guilt tactic.

As with science, theology is never settled either. Those who know and study the Bible have differing views and differing interpretations of the Biblical text. The section on what others have to say continues into the section on Christian responsibility. It is here that the meaning of worship is breached as are views on whether God is omnipresent or present in His creation. Respect must be shown for all points of view because they do present interesting and challenging concepts.

The Green New Deal has sparked another round of high visibility for environmentalist and climate change advocates. The introduction of this U. S. House resolution has highlighted the divide that exists in the climate change debate and seems to have further harden each side's resolve to hold their position. The chapter closes on some of the precepts of creation care that exist within scripture.

Christian stewardship is more than prudent care of earth and its resources. Some of the information in this chapter hopefully lets readers avoid letting the discussion on Christian stewardship become so singularly attached to the environment that other equally valid attributes are overlooked.

Go Forth and Multiply

God commanded His creation to go forth and multiply. If that is to be taken literally two elements surface. The first is that God must have designed the Earth to absorb a growing population. He provided abundant natural resources and gave mankind the mental power to innovate and invent. The second element is the abortion issue. How can humans multiply if we interfere with natural procreation?

This expansion of human activity has begun a discussion upon our impact on the planet on which we live. The political environment in the United States today is pushing and has pushed climate change to the level of an unrealistic state. The main culprit influencing climate change they suggest are we humans even questioning whether the extinction of humans would be a tragedy (May, 2018). The definition of climate is a weather pattern that is long term and geographically located. Long term has Biblical definitions that span human lifetime. Science has noted on one side that in our lifetime we probably cannot sense a change in the climate. We sense a change in the weather daily. The impetus of today's dialog is to change the definition of climate (Barber, 2018).

The world population has continued to grow since recorded time (World Population, n.d.). There have been times when disease or famine has decreased the population and times when the population has dramatically increased. There have been claims that we are running out of resources (Velson, 2017) for ages and have moved to new fevered heights of late (Berke, 2018). Remarkably, each time such a forecast is promoted we seem to adapt by ingenuity to extending our resources and life on Earth is sustained.

Be a Good Steward

Our sustainability sets in motion a new fear of fatalism. What to be alarmed about next and where's the data to substantiate that fear? It seems the new fear is climate change and not the depletion of our resources. To confuse this discussion, science itself has two postulates on the subject of climate change. Confusion allows sides to be taken without the interference of facts. The two sides of the climate debate do not agree on their conclusions and they cannot agree on which set of data are correct or applicable (Data). A review of passages from Genesis, especially Genesis 8, the Earth will never be destroyed and in verse 21 He states that He will not curse the ground anymore for man's sake. This seems to imply that the Earth will accommodate human kind and all that human kind brings to the Earth. Stewardship of God's resource is understood through passages such as these (Stewardship (theology), n.d.):

- "I am the Alpha and the Omega, the First and the Last, the Beginning and the End." (Revelation 22:13). Revelation 1:8 reiterates God is the beginning and the end.

This passage asserts that as God chose to create, He will also choose the ending. The following extractions of scripture may be leading to a certain conclusion not considered here though they may just as aptly apply to God's command over His creation and its destiny. Revelation 21:6 uses the terms Alpha and Omega, the beginning and the end. Psalms 104 is a chapter assailing God's care for His creation. God sets an example for stewardship and care. Revelation 1:17 quotes God as being the first and the last.

Isaiah 44:6, 48:12, and 41:4 repeat the message of God as being the first and the last. Isaiah 46:10 declares that He will accomplish all My good pleasure. Clearly these scriptures paint the picture of God being the One that decides the fate of our good Earth and not human kind. We do not know how our earthly behavior plays into God's decisions as only He knows. Colossians 1:16 reminds us that all things were created by Him and for Him. A pure statement from this is that what we have is not ours but His and it is His power and not ours that determines the future. This is not to suggest a laisse faire attitude towards our responsibility for caring.

We are reminded that "The earth is the Lord's, and everything in it, the world, and all who live in it." (Psalm 24:1) and "To the Lord your God belong the heavens, even the highest heavens, the earth and everything in it." (Deuteronomy 10:14).

Within a vast description of God being the Decider, God's Holiness is mentioned in Genesis 1:2 when the Spirit of God moved upon the face of the waters as a declaration of His power to create and eliminate. 2 Timothy

1:9 lets it be known that existence is not of our doing but is of His own purpose and grace. "He has saved us and called us to a holy life—not because of anything we have done but because of his own purpose and grace. This grace was given us in Christ Jesus before the beginning of time." If God created this space called Earth, then it demands the respect of Holy Ground.

These scriptures further show an expectation of stewardship for His creation. The repeated reference of God being the beginning and end in the two chapters of Revelations can be taken to mean that only God will decide the how and when of Earth's demise and not doomsayers or science.

A conclusion may be asserted that states that God has given human kind that ability to utilize His given resources for their benefit but has also given us an inherent wisdom to do so prudently and not wastefully.

God also vested humans with the ability to be creative. Several verses exemplify this characteristic where creativeness and steadfastness are encouraged. Each verse speaks to faith and an alternate approach to today's problems beyond fear. A comment on each is worthy space taken since these verses are at the heart of our current dilemma in society.

Yet We Survive

A good reason how it is that human kind has survived all of the perils of this world might lie in Philippians 4:6 ESV "Do not be anxious about anything, but in everything by prayer and supplication with thanksgiving let your requests be made known to God." Is this not saying that God answers prayers? James 1:5 remains a forever favorite in trying times where one only has to ask for wisdom, and it will be given to man liberally. Have past fears of our worldly demise been laid aside by God's grace of wisdom such that human kind's inventiveness and ingenuity became inspired by His grace to meet our challenges and succeed over them?

Only because of our frailty in faith have obstacles seemed insurmountable because Proverbs 3:5 ESV states the obvious solution. "Trust in the Lord with all your heart, and do not lean on your own understanding." Most of our challenges have been met with the zeal and courage of Philippians 4:13. "I can do all things through Him who strengthens me."

Matthew 7:7 says to ask and it shall be given; knock, and it will be opened to you. Proverbs 3:6 encourages us to acknowledge Him and He will set our path straight. These versus say that even if our attempts at stewardship may at times fail us, an answer still awaits us and by God's power we can correct our direction. History has recorded the many times human kind has failed in its duties of stewardship and respect. In the end and given time, these errors were corrected, and a new, wiser path pursued. Technology coupled with science have solved many of these problems. History also warns that some of what is seen as a solution today may not hold true tomorrow. Isaiah 28:29 expresses a word of caution about our own solutions to our problems. "All this also comes from the Lord Almighty, whose plan is wonderful, whose wisdom is magnificent." God has a plan. Isaiah 40:28 reminds us that His understanding no one can fathom. Simply, our solution might not be in God's plan at the present time. Our trust must be in His understanding of the bigger picture since we lack knowing the depth of His understanding of the long-term plan.

Yet we survive, even as fools despise wisdom and instruction (Proverb1:7). Today we endure an avalanche of information. Everyone too freely expresses their opinion in a way that closes the door to dialog and debate. "Fools find no pleasure in understanding but delight in airing their own opinions." Proverbs 18:2 | NIV. How often do we see this played out every day? The wisest seem to understand that "When pride comes, then comes disgrace, but with humility comes wisdom." Proverbs 11:2 | NIV. It is as if a fall must occur before reality sets in. The whole discussion on human kind's influence on the environment and even climate change would change for the better if the discussion was approached humbly. A willingness to understand another's position may not lead to being persuaded though at least each may part with the satisfaction of having been heard and not just listened to. One further thought to bear in mind is from Philippians 2:3 "Do nothing out of selfish ambition or vain conceit. Rather, in humility value others above yourselves." Ambition seems to be one of the overarching obstacles to today's discourse being conducted without humility. Discussion that has ambition as its main driver hammers shut any opportunity for understanding.

Doomsday Philosophy

Throughout time, humans have been presented with ominous forecasts of imminent doom. Politicians espouse the end being in the next decade unless drastic action is taking to save our planet. Others forecast wide spread food shortages if the population continues to grow to over 9 billion and possibly 11 billion which computer models are predicting. There seems to be little hope left for Earth's inhabitants. These same predictions have reoccurred throughout history; only the specific cause changes with time. Real calamities and disasters have occurred but not as the result of a prediction that someone made.

Biblical catastrophes happened because God made the prediction. Catastrophes since those times have been relatively uncategorized as to their cause. Some have been quite significant events ranging from World Wars to disease epidemics. The significance in how human kind has since responded has been much different from those events written about in the Bible. People were reactive to most of these events and not proactive in prevention. Reaction has been the mode of operation since time has long passed when catastrophic events were forecast for us. Each time we overcame the event and Biblical predictions are that we will continue this pattern until the ultimate end of Earth satisfies one last prediction and that is the return of Christ.

Though it is unwise to tempt fate or be foolish in our stewardship, two passages reaffirm that a power greater than ours can and will intervene if faithfully sought. Psalm 50:15 reminds us that God will deliver us if we call upon Him in the day of trouble. Mark 11:22-25 assures us that no mountain is insurmountable if we have faith in God. The passage reads beautifully: "And Jesus answered them, "Have faith in God. Truly, I say to you, whoever says to this mountain, 'Be taken up and thrown into the sea,' and does not doubt in his heart, but believes that what he says will come to pass, it will be done for him. Therefore, I tell you, whatever you ask in prayer, believe that you have received it, and it will be yours. And whenever you stand praying, forgive, if you have anything against anyone, so that your Father also who is in heaven may forgive you your trespasses."

Time is always a human obsession. God does not worry about our time or our impatience.

2 Peter 3:9 makes two profound statements in one verse: "The Lord is not slow to fulfill his promise as some count slowness, but is patient toward you, not wishing that any should perish, but that all should reach repentance." First is that the Lord is not slow. It is only our concept of time that leads us to consider such. Secondly, God does not wish any of us should perish. Perish though some of us may, it is not His wish. The discussion relative to the Fall sufficiently responds to the unfortunate happenings we may endure. 2 Peter simply expresses that God loves His people and wishes no harm to them. By this same measure, God has always responded to our needs when taken to Him in prayer.

Climate change, food shortages and overpopulating will be addressed in the same way past problems were resolved. Lest we remember, He is the first and the last, the beginning and the end. The only observable for we humans is time and that is a weakness of our own making. Some ask why it has taken years to resolve wars or years to solve disease epidemics. In God's time, though He does not count, resolutions unfold as He has chosen. It is we who are keeping time and our impatience that highlights how long something takes.

The sense is that no reasoned thought can permeate the bombardment of fatalistic forecasts that are used to push a position. Time will come when this passage will be the test. "For I will give you a mouth and wisdom, which none of your adversaries will be able to withstand or contradict" Luke 21:15. It's a recurring theme that out of all of the rhetoric comes a message that cannot be contradicted nor withstood.

What Others Say

In "What should be the Christian's response to this issue?", an article by faculty members at Master's University (Dennis Englin, 2017), the authors state: "Thus it appears that in God's creative wisdom He has made an earth that is resilient to major changes in temperature or changes in atmospheric gas composition.". Their article provides charts and graphs of data for one hundred years to explain how the earth has returned to an equilibrium temperature after periods of both cold and warm. They use Genesis 1:1 as a point where science and religion agree and that is the "beginning" included both earth and heaven. An agreement is also accepted that the earth will come to an end involving heat. They quote Job 5:7 to say that man is by nature destructive and his destructive way needs to be controlled and corrected.

Theologians and Christian practitioners have also taken different sides in the climate/environmental debate. An honor's thesis (Rocklin, 2011) titled "Dueling Dualisms: Christian Theology in Response to Global Climate Change" focused on the works of two writers with different opinions about creation and the Biblical statements on the world.

Rocklin first discussed the work of Sallie McFague who argues that ecological, evolutionary sensibility can be religious. She focuses on interpretation of God's statement that His Creation is "good". Genesis 1:10 ESV: "God called the dry land Earth, and the waters that were gathered together he called Seas. And God saw that it was good. "The word "saw" is how the English Standard Version interprets the text.

Implying as she does that since God does not state it is good for Him nor good for man then all of nature is good and not just for the goodness of human kind. She further states that our complicity towards global warming is in our consumer culturalism. This falls in line with several modern positions that suggest God is nature and therefore the whole earth is God and anything we do to the earth is by association being done to God. Along with this train of thought are other writings that debate whether God actually gave man dominion other the earth and all that is in it.

Rocklin does present other published thoughts on the human and Christian concept of earth's treatment, but he uses writings from Gordon Kaufman to counter McFague to some degree. Kaufman states that humans have evolved to the point that they may create their own demise rather than God doing so. Kaufman is identified as a progressive Christian. Both present ideas that are contrary to holding the Word as being what it is. If the Bible states that God will end life on earth, it will be God and not humans. Matthew 24:35 ESV: "Heaven and earth will pass away, but my words will not pass away."

Another paper is more direct in the liberal or progressive view of the human, earth and God relationship. Joshua Martin (Martin, 2009) makes the following statement in his abstract about his honors paper objective: "…an endorsement of a panentheistic, pneumatological, and pro-environmental evangelical framework that recognizes the pervasive presence of the divine in all life forms. This solution will build upon the liberal evangelical treatment of the environment isolated from the problematic notion of human ontology possessed by conservative evangelicals…" This would seem contrary to Genesis 1:26-28 King James Version (KJV)

[26] And God said, let us make man in our image, after our likeness: and let them have dominion over the fish of the sea, and over the fowl of the air, and over the cattle, and over all the earth, and over every creeping thing that creepeth upon the earth.

[27] So God created man in his own image, in the image of God created he him; male and female created he them.

[28] And God blessed them, and God said unto them, be fruitful, and multiply, and replenish the earth, and subdue it: and have dominion over the fish of the sea, and over the fowl of the air, and over every living thing that moveth upon the earth.

Clearly God's intention was for man to subdue the earth and replenish it. Two points are made. The first is God gave man permission to use the resources of the earth. The second point is the directive to replenish. I think this is the mandate to be good stewards of our resources and not wasteful of them. The directives on stewardship will follow in the discussion on caring for God's creation and the human responsibility to do so.

The following passage raises questions. Genesis 8:22 ESV: "While the earth remains, seedtime and harvest, cold and heat, summer and winter, day and night, shall not cease." The starting question on while the earth remains can only be answered later in scripture. If the return of Jesus Christ to earth begins the end of earth, then clearly earth and humans will remain on earth until that time. This is another statement that humans will not create their own destruction. Another question whose answer can be assumed from this verse is that earth that we know will continue to be as we see it now until Christ returns. This lays into the theory that our actions will somehow create a continually deteriorating earth. This verse suggests otherwise.

Christian Responsibility

God created humanity in God's own image…and said to them, "Be fertile and multiply; fill the earth and master it. Take care of the fish of the sea, the birds in the sky, and everything crawling on the ground." Then God said, "I now give to you all the plants on the earth that yield seeds and all the trees whose fruit produces its seeds within it. These will be your food. To all wildlife, to all the birds in the sky, and to everything crawling on the ground—to everything that breathes—I give all the green grasses for food." And that's what happened. God saw everything he had made: it was supremely good. Genesis 1:27-31 CEB

The Rev. Rebekah Simon-Peter is quoted as saying "You can't love God and ignore the Earth." (Passi-Klaus, 2015). One premise of Simon-Peter is that we may fill the world with humans to the point of pushing everything else into extinction. She refers to God having first given the command to go forth and multiply to the birds and the fish (Genesis 1:20-23). Therefore,

God spoke first to his non-human creation. She further cites a statistic (not referenced) that between 200 to 2000 species go extinct every year. She further states that we cannot separate our life with God from our life on His earth.

The movement of holding the environment and our earth as some sort of religion dates to pagan history. It is holding an ideological passion more reverent than our Creator. The ancients may have had an excuse for worshiping the landscape that gave them substance. Christianity had not spread around the globe and even today continues it that crusade. In contrast to Simon-Peter, having been presented with another interpretation of the Word, some theologians would argue that we should be cautious about being too zealous in confusing stewardship responsibilities with worship.

A climate change enthusiast, meteorologist and Christian Paul Douglas states, "It's true that all knowledge is relative; science is never "settled" and one never quite reaches solid bedrock. There's always a new observation, a new discovery, a radical theory, more testing to do. We look at the universe through a pinhole as God gradually reveals himself to us." (Douglas, 2017). Thus, we need to understand that scientific inquiry is supposed to generate a ream of explorative conclusions.

What should be our priority? Worship is to honor with extravagant love and extreme submission (Webster's Dictionary,1828). We should know our only priority of worship and it is not our earthly domain. Recall previous reminders that stewardship is a responsibility and not our focus of worship. The following quote is worth contemplating: "True worship, in other words, is defined by the priority we place on *who* God is in our lives and *where* God is on our list of priorities. True worship is a matter of the heart expressed through a lifestyle of holiness. Thus, if your lifestyle does not express the beauty of holiness through an extravagant or exaggerated love for God, and you do not live in extreme or excessive submission to God…" (Kennebrew, 2012).

"Take care lest your heart be deceived, and you turn aside and serve other gods and worship them; then the anger of the LORD will be kindled against you, and he will shut up the heavens, so that there will be no rain, and the land will yield no fruit, and you will perish quickly off the good land that the LORD is giving you (Deut. 11:16)." Some theological positions bring the above Deuteronomy quote to bear on letting our worship focus slip from the one and only priority. Therefore, it could be that this warning is not about humans aggravating or exacerbating climate change but that our worship focus is in err and climate change is the outcome. Treat the illness and not the symptom. "God Wants His People Exclusively to Worship Him and Him Alone!" (American Patriotism and Christian Worship, 2016).

Aside from our focus on the direction of our worship, the Christian community is split on word definitions. The NBC article "The gospel of climate change: Green pastors bringing environmentalism to evangelicals" (Sacks, 2018) provides insight how the interpretation of the word "dominion" in Genesis is defined and thus generates differing positions. Other words generate a cross pollination of definitions as well. Words and terms such as "creation care", 1 Thessalonians 5:21 (prove all things…), embrace either God or God's creation, and catastrophic anthropogenic global warming become obstacles to circumventing circular fallacies where no common ground can be found. The debate continues in a never-ending circle and no consensus can be reached.

The Green New Deal

The media and the headlines are bustling over the introduction of a progressive resolution in Congress called the Green New Deal. The insinuation of the resolution is that fossil fuels are evil, the major cause of climate change and that the end of life on earth is near. Approximately ten to twelve years out it says. Little thought has been given in the resolution to the ramifications to many of its proposals. Of particular note would be the impact on the quality of life for millions of Americans if automobiles, reliable power grids, employment in energy producing and manufacturing businesses and on health care. All of this seems appropriate to sacrifice to save the planet. God has given human kind the ability to improve upon His creation and to improve their standard of living. America has used this ability to move from subsistence existence to our current standard of living and the outcome has been longer, healthier lifespans for the most part.

The headline from the Christian Headline "The Green New Deal: Government Is Not Our Savior" (John Stonestreet, 2019) is a good indication as to how some in the Christian community are accepting the concepts in the Green New Deal. 2 Thessalonians 3:10 responds adequately to the concept of a living wage to those unable or unwilling to work. If none work, neither shall they eat. Jonah Goldberg of the National Review goes so far as to say the plan is dangerous.

He continues saying "The proposal, like every worldview, answers at least two questions: (1) what's wrong with the world, and (2) how can we fix it? On both counts, the Green New Deal is profoundly out-of-touch with reality. Rather than human evil, the breakdown of the family, or the compromise of morality, the Green New Deal identifies the modern economy as the problem and promises to dismantle it without offering any viable replacement."

The Christian Post had more to say about Christian alignment with the concepts in the Green New Deal. Writer Chuck Bentley had the following to say on the matter:

"Genesis 2:15 says, "The Lord God took the man and put him in the Garden of Eden to work it and take care of it." Adam was given a stewardship responsibility in the garden before the Fall of Creation. Man was placed here to work and manage the beautiful world God created.

But it doesn't stop there. Throughout God's Word we learn that we are to faithfully manage more than just natural resources but our time, talents, finances, our children, and the gospel as well. Stewardship is the Lord's way of restoring all that is broken in the world. More on this below.

Second question, "do we have to become socialists to preserve our natural resources'? Answer: No. In fact, it is faulty logic to believe that the public sector will be better stewards of anything than those in the private sector. However, I do agree with you that what is being touted as the solution to potential environmental catastrophe, the <u>Green New Deal (GND)</u>, is cause for concern and a great leap forward towards a dangerous form of government if the legislation is enacted as law." (Bentley, 2019)

Bentley introduces the broader Biblical expectations of us concerning stewardship. Managing our time, talents, finances, family and the gospel. These further commands from scripture get overlooked in the zest of favoring stewardship of the environment over the other equally important parts vested in us as God's creation. It should be noted that the U. S. Conference of Catholic Bishops have supported several of the concepts the Green New Deal propose, and they have opposed measures the current U. S. government is implementing regarding environmental legislation and positions. Thus far, the congressional non-binding resolution has been mostly shrugged off as a wish list of ideas and not a serious proposition. It is lacking in any proposals on how to accomplish their ambitious expectations. As its details are more adequately reviewed there will certainly be more comment on it and the Christian perspective will undoubtedly be part of future discussions.

Creation Care

Several quarters push narratives and to get the Christian buy-in to some of those narratives, they use the stewardship aspect of Biblical directives. As highlighted above, Biblical stewardship extends beyond stewardship of the earth and the environment. There are certain principles that Christians should respond to since God did create all that we have and what we have is a gift from Him. Thus, we should treat His offerings with the same respect that He expects we pay to Him as our creator.

God created the universe for His glory as all systematic theology books reiterate. Therefore, God owns all of creation. If this is accepted, then the resources on earth are not ours to squander or abuse. God also loves His creation. His actions throughout Biblical history in His treatment of human kind more than shows His love for all His creation. God values His creation and stated so in saying what He saw was "good". God sustains His creation. Numerous passages listed below in summary fashion show His ability to sustain His works. Job 26:7-9, 11-14 and Psalms 104:24-25 in particular highlight His sustaining character for creation. 2 Chronicles 7:13-14 speaks of God redeeming and healing not only His people but also their land. Psalms 104 continues the message of renewing the face of the earth in verses 29-30. Given these qualities that God shares upon His creation, there should be sufficient arguments that we do have the responsibility to care diligently for the gifts (resources) God has given us. With this guidance, Christians can say they share the same concern over abuse of our planet and all those things within it. A caveat must be in this discussion that stewardship must take into consideration the collateral impact of certain environmental movements upon other components of God's creation. Namely, the one most important component must be the impact of these movements upon our fellow humans. A movement to radically abandon our current use of resources will inevitably transfer further burdens upon those with the least ability, economically or physically, to adapt. Another chapter will address charity, the poor and our responsibility to the least among us. This precept is currently grossly overlooked by proponents of climate change and a green economy. The solution is in continued education and impressing upon society God's commandments to care for His creation.

Caring for God's Creation	Substantiating Scriptures	
Genesis 1:1,31	Hebrews 1:3	Job 26:7-9,11-14
2 Chronicles 7:13-14	Psalm 65:9-13	Colossians 1:20
Psalm 104:24-25	Colossians 1:17	Nehemiah 9:6
Psalm 104:10-14	Psalm 104:29-30	Luke 12:6-7

ABORTION AND THE WORD

They Push Harder

There is no better time than the present to delve into the subject of abortion and the Christian position. On January 22, 2019 the Governor of New York signed a bill allowing abortion right up to the time of birth. What was even more appalling to many was that the legislators and guests at the signing actually cheered the signing as if it were a proud accomplishment. (O'Kane, 2019).

It was not enough to have New York relishing in their great liberal accomplishment but also to witness a similar unsuccessful feat transpire in Virginia a few days later. To add to the turmoil, Governor Ralph Northam provided an extremely detailed description of how the legislation would allow for a baby to be aborted after it was born if the family and medical advisor so wished. (North, 2019).

Needless to say, an abundance of criticism has subsequently followed. It is best summarized by a National Public Radio interview between commentator Ari Shapiro and guest Sarah McCammon (Shapiro, 2019). Her closing comment predicts what lays ahead in the political and public domain: "…we're likely to see more of these debates in the months to come. For example, in New York, they just passed a law allowing abortions after 24 weeks to protect a woman's life or health. And with all the changes in the U.S. Supreme Court, there's a big tug of war over abortion rights-conservatives wanting to restrict them, liberals wanting to expand them. And we're going to see more of that in the months to come." Certainly, more to come with the word "infanticide" being so closely attached to the discussion. (Appell, 2019).

As the sides on the abortion debate stake out their advocacy and defense, they invariably bring Christianity into the picture. There is a recognition within a public discussion like abortion that the Christian community in the United States still has influence. For years, the LGBQT and abortion community have lobbied religious organizations and denominations to liberalize their positions on homosexuality and abortion. They have accomplished a degree of success. Much of what that is presented in this chapter shows that the process has been ongoing for many years. The push towards liberalizing religion in America is not that new.

The liberal push has been reinvigorated recently with the changes in Congress created by the 2018 election. Almost immediately after the House majority turning Democrat, the liberal wing of that party began exerting its new-found political power. The Congressional changes were followed within weeks by New York passing its late term abortion bill referred to above and Virginia attempting to pass a similar piece of legislation. The United States is one of seven developed countries that allows late term abortion; abortion after twenty weeks of development. Medical science has now been able to show infant survivability outside the womb as early as twenty-two weeks with success.

Twenty-five states have limits on abortion after or close to the twenty-week mark. Another twenty-five and Washington, D. C. have no late term abortion limits. With such a split in state regulations, it is easy to see why the debate has moved into the federal court. Though bills have been introduced to limit late term abortion at the federal level, none have been able to cross the legislative finish line. Earlier attempts, if they were successfully passed by Congress, faced the veto threat from the Executive Branch. Now that the Executive Branch would likely support legislation restricting late term abortions, it is Congress that presents the barrier.

Christians and particularly Christian leaders face a dilemma. What does the Bible say or not say? As will be seen by the material highlighted as an example of the discussion in this chapter, it is often what the Bible does not say on the abortion issue that swings the most leverage. The most prevalent tactic that appears in the debate is the use of various logical fallacies since emphatic Biblical statements do not exist. Therefore, this chapter first discusses the use of logical fallacies witnessed in today's discussion and concludes with the suggestions from Christian writers and students on how Christians may wish to respond to the debate.

Omission Makes It True

One of the most apparent phenomena observed in the discussion of Christianity and its position on abortion is the use of logical fallacies in the dialog. A logical fallacy is defined as a flaw in reasoning. Interestingly, the definition also includes that fallacies are often very sneakily used by politicians and the media to fool people. Merriam-Webster includes in the definition that it is a plausible argument using false or invalid inference. It is this later definition that will be highlighted in this chapter. An excellent source listing logical fallacy is an open source course at the University of Texas, El Paso; http://utminers.utep.edu/omwilliamson/ENGL1311/fallacies.htm.

Scott Klusendorf makes this statement in an opinion piece on abortion and women's right to choose: "Abortion advocates are correct that the Bible does not specifically mention abortion, but what's the best explanation for its silence? The hidden (and undefended) premise in the argument advanced by Ward, Bigelow, and Simmons is that whatever the Bible doesn't condemn it condones. It's easy to see that this premise is flawed, since it leads to some absurd conclusions. The Bible does not expressly condemn many things, including racial discrimination against blacks, killing abortion doctors as a means of fighting abortion, and lynching homosexuals, and yet few people would argue that these acts are morally justified. We know, in fact, that they are wrong by inference." (Klusendorf, 2019). How well does this statement fit Webster's definition?

In observing how the abortion debate is attempting to bring Christians into the conversation, my education training brought the principles of fallacies into mind. It seems that the proponents of women's right to choose and abortion are well schooled in their use as well. Some of the observed uses and tactics cannot be ignored because they can be effective persuaders of public opinion.

Frequently Used Fallacies

One of the first observed is the <u>If-by-whiskey</u> argument that supports both sides of an issue by using terms that are selectively emotionally sensitive. Emotion is the key word in this fallacy. People quickly align their positions on a subject to their emotions about it. They gravitate towards being passionate about some subjects because they have a personal attachment to the issue or have been brought up in culture that supports their view. The power of attaching an emotion to a cause can be alarming. It entrenches an opinion into an almost immovable point that debate, and understanding cannot overcome. There need not be a winner in a debate, but clarity in each other's feeling on the matter. The feeling can come from emotional attachment, from concrete science or from experience. Since this sense is real to person holding it, they may not be persuadable to the other's position.

<u>Cherry picking</u> is the suppression of evidence or providing incomplete evidence. It is an act of pointing at individual cases or data that seem to confirm a position, while ignoring a significant portion of related cases or data that may contradict that position. This is too frequently thrown into the mix in the media. The only comments the public is given access to are those that simply support the message being conveyed by the messenger. There are usually several other pieces of evidence that are present that might cause one to pause and question the data set being presented. Yet, the peripheral evidence is withheld knowing well that it would weaken the intent of the original supporting data.

The public is only presented with Bible quotes that support the claim that abortion is not a Biblical issue. The cherry-picking name is very appropriate to this technique. It is often incorporated with two other fallacies that further antagonize the painting of a more holistic picture of the Biblical position on a topic. The frequency with which the <u>Argument from ignorance</u> is used is appalling. The ignorance argument is an appeal to ignorance, *argumentum ad ignorantiam*. Its foundation is to assume that a claim is true because it has not been or cannot be proven false, or vice versa. This is convincing since it denies a counter argument the chance of any validity. Numerous arguments that use Bible scripture for supporting abortion use this tactic. Since no scriptures exist to say abortion is wrong, then abortion must be acceptable. What they say may be correct in one sense, but omission does not by itself mean condoning.

Cherry picking is secondly coupled with the <u>Bandwagon fallacy</u>. It is also known at the Argument from Common Sense, Argumentum ad Populum. It is the fallacy of arguing that because "everyone," "the people," or "the majority" (or someone in power who has widespread backing) supposedly thinks or does something, it must therefore be true and right. There is power in numbers when it comes to public persuasion. It is akin to the mob mentality. However, Christians know that following the crowd is often bad and following the Word is the more stable ground. Pro-Choice advocates like to present crowds as a means of saying they have the majority's blessing and therefore they're position is correct. The marches and demonstrations are the means that they use to reinforce their territory. It is an intimidation tactic that blatantly says that for your position to hold credence, you're going to have to take us all on and that is a challenge. The Bandwagon fallacy has been successfully deployed many times throughout history and was no less evident than at the hearing and crucifixion of Jesus.

Lastly, two fallacies are extremely prominent in the abortion debate. They are the <u>evidence of absence and the fallacy of omission</u>. Absence states that evidence of any kind that suggests that something is missing or that it does not exist. This follows the trend of repeating that since it is not said or mentioned directly in the Bible then its absence means that it is not a Biblical issue. The aphorism is absence of evidence is not evidence of absence. It is wise to consider that evidence may exist but in such a succinct form that it does not appear as evidence. There are many scriptures that can used to support the protection of fetal life as if it is breathed into life if one wishes to so connect them to the abortion debate.

The <u>circular argument and the fallacy of omission</u> are very troublesome tactics since neither permits an escape to redirect the focus of an argument. I believe God exists. Why? Because the Bible says He does. Why should you believe the Bible? Because the Bible says it is the Word of God. The loop is continuous and always returns to original statement as proof that all further statements are true because it says so. Pro-choice advocates use this in their presentation of their cause. Because it is hard to disprove the starting point, it is hard to disprove the remaining points.

The <u>Fallacies of omission</u> occur because the logician leaves out necessary material in an argument or misdirects others from the missing information. I am only going to show you what supports my position and withhold everything that exists but weakens my position. In the discussion further in this chapter, several opinion pieces will be discussed as if they are Biblically sound but omit a whole cadre of information that would destroy that tenet.

It is important to understand that there is a strategy that is being used to misdirect and misguide the Christian community into supporting the abortion cause and this strategy is not so innocent as it appears on the surface. Truly, the Pro-Choice movement is professional, and they know how to raise doubts in the minds of committed Christians. It is that they use professional techniques that is so disappointing and unfair to a public that is not wise to their ways. Entire Christian denominations and assemblies that should not fall so easily into their trap are joining their bandwagon on completely artificial premises on what being a Christian is. It is to say; a sin is a sin.

The Arguments

Ireland has had a strong Catholic background and much of their legislation over the years has been tied closely to the Catholic doctrine. In the news lately is their move to a more liberalized government stance on abortion. The Irish Pro-Choice movement has been very critical of the Catholic influence in governmental decisions. Atheist Ireland was very vocal in 2018 and frequently used Bible passages to support abortion law relaxation in Ireland by a repeal of their 8th Amendment. (Hamill, 2018)

The same Biblical passages used to support abortion are similarly used to defend life beginning at conception. Lynn Copeland, Editor & President, The Genesis Publishing Group listed several passages suggesting life begins at conception if not before in an article titled "What God's Word Says about Abortion". (Copeland, 2019). This article dates to 1985 which demonstrates that this debate has been around for many years as has been the mission on both sides to weave religion into the arguments. The abortion debate in the United States has been taking place since the 7-4 U. S. Supreme Court ruling Roe vs Wade of 22 January, 1973. This ruling tied a State's jurisdiction to the last trimester of pregnancy. In 1992 the Planned Parenthood vs. Casey ruling extended Roe to a woman's right to an abortion until fetal viability which had been previously defined as a fetus's ability to survive outside the mother's womb. (Roe v. Wade, 2019).

Some of the passages that have been used to support the beginning of life is at conception are listed below. These are often cited to counter the argument that focuses on Genesis where life begins or began when God breathed life into Adam: The passages are (Copeland, 2019):

"The babies jostled each other within her." (Genesis 25:22)

"When Elizabeth heard Mary's greeting, the baby leaped in her womb." (Luke 1:41)

"Before I formed you in the womb I knew you, before you were born I set you apart." (Jeremiah 1:5)

For You created my inmost being; You knit me together in my mother's womb… Your eyes saw my unformed body. All the days ordained for me were written in Your book before one of them came to be. (Psalm 139:13,16)

"Your hands shaped me and made me . . . Did You not clothe me with skin and flesh and knit me together with bones and sinews? You gave me life." (Job 10:8–12)

This is what the Lord says—He who made you, who formed you in the womb. (Isaiah 44:2)

"Did not He who made me in the womb make them? Did not the same One form us both within our mothers?" (Job 31:15)

"I have set before you life and death, blessings and curses. Now choose life, so that you and your children may live." (Deuteronomy 30:19)

Using Old Testament Reasoning

The passage in Exodus 21:22-25 (Exodus 21, 2019) has often been used to demonstrate that abortion was an acceptable practice in Biblical times. This passage suggests using the principle of penalty for harming a woman and/or a fetus or both. It implies by the penalty applied that a woman's life is valued as a person while the fetus is valued as property. This one passage has divided Biblical scholars. Supporting the use of an Old Testament scripture for evaluating the morality of abortion is the verse where Jesus states "Do not think that I have come to abolish the Law or the Prophets; I have come not to abolish but to fulfil." This passage is argued to validate an Old Testament practice or covenant being relevant in the New Covenant era. There is room to debate whether Matthew 5:17 was a carte blanche approval to accept everything in the Old Testament Covenants as also New Covenant laws. Some argue the New Covenant replaced the Old and the fulfilling that is referenced applies to only the Old Testament prophecies of the Messiah coming to earth.

Besides the debate over the meaning of various passages is the intent of some of the same passages as it relates to when life begins. The debate becomes even more convoluted in this discussion. The questions are when does life begin and how does life begin. Is it at conception or when a heartbeat can be heard or is it at some other time? What is breathing life into a creation?

This could be a figurative description more so than a physical description. When God breathes life into any life form is unknown except to God. It is possible that the breath of life is the instant of conception. Arguments are put forth that squelching a life at any stage of development is in essence murder. "Life is holy, pure and inviolable, and we must respect it as we respect God, the giver of life. Throughout the whole Bible it is clear that God knows all things, also that which is to come, and has known this from eternity. In this way He has also always known each person, each life – even before conception." (Christianity, 2019). The article "What is the Christian view on abortion?" in Active Christianity includes this conclusion on to what is a Christian's view on abortion: "So what is a Christian view on abortion? Christianity is based on faith in the Almighty God, and in His creating power, both in natural and in spiritual things. The Bible, being the Word of God, is the basis for how we conduct our lives. Our trust is in God, the Almighty Creator, who knows all things – also the lives of those yet unborn. We, His creation, are called to live before Him in reverence and awe, with full, unwavering faith in His boundless love, goodness and wisdom. Any decision made with God brings rest and peace. We believe that many lives would have been spared if God had been sought before these decisions were made." (Christianity, 2019).

American Right to Life (America Right to Life, 2019) has been a very vocal critic of the abortion movement. There work is set against the backdrop of the many that support abortion. As there can be innumerable examples of publications attempting to show that the Bible does not condemn abortion so therefore it must be acceptable, there are others who choose to demonstrate that these same passages are just as useful in showing that abortion is not acceptable. As an example, a common argument is evident in an article by Brian Bolton, well known member of Freedom from Religion. The article is titled "God is so Not Pro-Life" (Bolton, 2019). Bolton cites ten incidences in the Bible where God or His delegate annihilated entire cities or populations which included children and babies and unborn babies. Bolton implies that since God can destroy all these people that God is not pro-life and therefore the connotation is that God really isn't concerned about death by abortion. Bolton's use of these stories is typical of pro-abortion advocates using only the part of a story that supports their position. The context of the stories cited by Bolton describe events before and after these events but since they are not germane to his position, they are omitted. No mention is made of the reason God took the action he did against these populations. No mention is made that God has always presented Himself as being just and more than willing to discipline when His commandments are broken. Instead, the Bolton article chose to use the instances he cites as an example that God is more than willing to kill and by extension approves abortion. Surprisingly, Bolton did not use the Noah story.

The American Right to Life countered some pro-abortion proponents by explaining Mosaic law and the Code of Hammurabi. (Corporate, 2017). Excerpts of Code are frequently used in pro-abortion support to show historical treatment of the fetus as property and the mother as a person having rights. Exodus 21 is again much used repetitively. The Mosaic law, as used then, was demonstrating discipline to the individual and provided instructions whereas the Code of Hummurabi espoused the "eye for an eye" philosophy. Mosaic law was established by God while the Code was enacted by the sixth Babylonian king, Hammurabi. The national god of Babylonia was Marduk. There is considerable distance between the authority of God and the authority of a Babylonian king that did not worship God.

The following passages have been presented by some as evidence that the Bible does recognize the unborn fetus as a person. Jesus was a full-term baby that further exemplifies that from conception, the breathing and born baby's life was started upon conception.

"Behold, the virgin shall be with *child*, and bear a Son." –Mat. 1:23

"Rebekah his wife conceived [and] the *children* [Jacob and Esau, the most famous twins in history] struggled together within her." –Moses, Genesis 25:22

"Behold, you shall conceive and bear a son [Samson]. Now drink no wine or similar drink… for the *child* shall be a Nazirite to God from the womb…" –Judges 13:7

"...a woman with *child* [then] *gives birth...*" Exodus 21:22

"He will also be filled with the Holy Spirit, even from his mother's womb. And... the babe [little Johnnie] leaped in her womb..." –Luke 1:15, 41

"Before I formed you in the womb I knew *you...*" –Jeremiah 1:5 (Corporate, 2017)

Killing of the innocent is referred to as murder. There is no escaping how many different ways Exodus 21:22 is interpreted. American Right to Life presents it this way: "... is the first fetal homicide law and concerns the child harmed during a separate assault. Pro-abortion theologians wrongly interpret this passage to refer to miscarriage, and only if the woman also dies is the penalty then life for life. But the passage distinguishes between the baby who survives the assault and the baby who dies. The meaning turns on whether the woman has a miscarriage or gives birth prematurely. And the Hebrew verb used is NOT that for miscarriage. Therefore, the passage imposes only a fine on the criminal who accidentally causes a premature birth, but the punishment is life for life if the baby then dies. This shows that God equated the life of the unborn with that of the born, and abortion with murder." (Corporate, 2017).

The argument about life beginning with the first breath is countered by Biblical scripture emphasizing life is in the blood. These two passages provide a different perspective on when life begins: "For the life of the flesh is in the blood" –Lev. 17:11 and do not "sin against innocent blood" –1 Sam. 19:5. The arguments proceed with the necessity of evacuating the airways of premature babies who are clearly alive but unable to breath without intervention. The blood is flowing, the premature baby is clearly alive, and it has not yet taken a breath. As agreeable this argument may be to Pro-Life advocates, it is seldom recognized as a valid point to counter the Genesis story of God breathing life into Adam.

Christians are reminded not to judge. Christians can judge; judge righteously. A distinction needs to be made between being judgmental and judging. The abortion movement criticizes and accuses Christian of judging those who have had abortions the same as they use this point about the Biblical view on homosexuality. Historically, there was a stigma attached to out-of-wedlock children and abortion. Christians need to be cognizant of history. Regarding the Christian practice of judging when necessary, these three verses provide the dictate using the words of Jesus: "You have rightly judged." Luke 7:43; "Do not judge according to appearance, but judge with righteous judgment." John 7:24; "Why, even of yourselves, do you not judge what is right?" Luke 12:56-57. The Bible does not contradict itself by saying "judge rightly" and "judge not". Without God's permission to judge, how could Christians establish any principles to guide their Christian life? Christians must judge many things that are blatantly and clearly wrongs against humanity.

The issue in this discussion is how it is that if Christians have strong convictions against abortion that the position of the church, whatever church it may be, isn't addressed more from the pulpit. In a Billy Graham Evangelistic Association article by Jerry Prevo titled "Why Do Many Pastors Avoid Warning against Homosexuality and Abortion?" (Prevo, 2019) He quotes researcher George Barna's statistic that 90 percent of pastors recognizes the Bible speaks of the issue of abortion and homosexuality but fewer than 10 percent actually teach what the Bible says about them. The later part of Prevo's article addresses the Christian and Biblical position on abortion. His key points are David's announcement that God has formed him from conception (Psalm 139:13, 16,) and Exodus 20:13 which states that you shall not murder. Both arguments are frequently used in the Pro-Life rebuttals to abortion. Prevo focuses on why pastors are not advancing these points to their congregations more often if at all. He acknowledges the politics of breaching the subject that a local minister must overcome. He provides several good reasons why preaching the truth from God's Word is in the best interest of even those that may take offense. He closes with advice to clergy: "Every one of us as pastors and preachers needs to sit down and have a serious evaluation of our preaching. Are we preaching the Word—convincing, rebuking, exhorting with all longsuffering? Or are we shrinking back from preaching what Almighty God says?"

The Question of Truth

Dr. Alex McFarland made this statement about humans innately knowing right from wrong. "Phrases like 'self-evident truth,' 'higher law' or 'the laws of nature and nature's God'—these were terms used to describe the awareness of right or wrong known to all people," McFarland continued. "Natural law doesn't mean that people always do what is right. But deep down, in our conscience, people really do know what's right. This has been amply documented by many scholars, persuasively arguing that humans are a species uniquely 'hardwired' with the ability to know right from wrong." (McFarland, 2019).

How is it that this hardwired human ability is not able to better govern debates over subjects that should seem rather clear cut regarding right and wrong? Certainly, the killing or destroying of life should resonate rather strongly the feelings of right or wrong. Abortion can be looked at as the taking of life and therefore the emotion and feeling about it should be clear. What convolutes or diminishes the feeling is the use of a supplanted reason for the action such a woman's right to choose. Admittedly, the emotion and feeling over a "right to choose" something is not as heart tugging as saying you're going to extinguish a life.

Ken Gewertz presents an interesting taking on how the situation governs if not overrides our inherited sense of right or wrong. He makes an interesting note about religion's role in providing rules when no other rules apply. In a Harvard Gazette article, he writes: "The fact that humans have done horrible things is undeniable. The universality is in the judging part, not in the doing part," he said.

Where religion and culture do make a difference is in how people judge situations. For example, in a famous essay, "A Defense of Abortion," moral philosopher Judith Jarvis Thomson presents a hypothetical situation in which a person wakes up in bed and finds he has had his circulatory system connected with that of a famous violinist. He is told that the two of them must remain connected for nine months or else the violinist will die. Is it permissible to unplug oneself from the violinist even though doing so would cause his death?

The clear majority of people asked this question say that it is permissible to unplug oneself, even though the difference between this situation and pregnancy is difficult to articulate.

"Religion gives you rules that don't apply when they are removed from the specific situation," Hauser said. (Gewertz, 2007).

The following excerpt by Lin Edwards in Medical Xpress draws from the work of Paul Bloom, professor of psychology at the Infant Cognition Center at Yale University in Connecticut. "The currently prevailing theory on human development is that human beings start their lives with a "moral blank state," but new research contradicts this view. The researchers have found babies as young as six months old already make moral judgments, and they think we may be born with a moral code hard-wired into our brains." (Edwards, 2010)

Even psychological research is accepting that our hardwired understanding of right and wrong is in us well before we are fully capable of learning right and wrong from someone else. Recent research on this subject seems to debunk the "born with a blank slate" ideology when it comes to moral judgement.

If a moral judgement ability exists in humans in some genetic framework, how is it that people can take such hard-lined positions on subjects that should be easily agreed upon? An article in *Science* describes the question of emotions and morality existing together. What calculations does the mind go through in a dilemma and do we possess a stronger willingness to let our conscience mind override our sub-conscience mind? "Daily life is peppered with moral decisions. Some are so automatic that they fail to register—like holding the door for a mother struggling with a stroller or resisting a passing urge to elbow the guy who cut you in line at Starbucks. Others chafe a little more, like deciding whether to give money to a figure rattling a cup of coins on a darkening evening commute. A desire to help, a fear of danger, and a cost-benefit analysis of the contents of my wallet; these gut reactions and reasoned arguments all swirl beneath conscious awareness." (Davis, 2016). The Stanford Encyclopedia of Philosophy (Moral Reasoning, 2018) discusses our reasoning as tracking both explicitly and tacitly. It discusses at length how though we are called upon to reason morally, we do it badly.

It is worth understanding that a person's position on abortion is a reality to them. Reasoning will not work in changing their minds. Even though we are hardwired for moral reasoning, we have an abundance of resources that can come into play to override our sub-conscience response. With this fact known, the abortion debate from the Pro-Life side should adapt and approach the wrongness of abortion from a practical level rather than an emotional level. Dare say that economics, population dynamics, America's future, brain power depletion and a host of other arguments could enter into the discussion. Above all, abandon the blame game. Literature is overflowing with the mental issues emanating from the decision to have an abortion. Separate the discussion from "freedom to choose" and focus on the "freedom to leave a heritage". The cost-benefit calculation has to favor the "heritage" by an amount far exceeding the right to choose. It is hoped that the dialog can transition into a phase beyond "rights" and "freedom" to a pragmatic discussion on how best to serve the God that created us and gifted us with the tools to do right from a very early age if not from the moment of conception.

Current Activity on the Abortion Debate

The Department of Health and Human Services announced Friday, February 22, 2019 that a new rule was finalized, forbidding "the use of Title X funds to perform, promote, refer for, or support abortion as a method of family planning." "Pursuant to Congressional mandate, family participation is to be encouraged, particularly in services involving adolescents. And, from the start, Congress was clear that Title X funds cannot be used to support abortion," stated HHS. (Gryboski, 2019)

"This final rule ensures that grants and contracts awarded under this program fully comply with the statutory program integrity requirements, thereby fulfilling the purpose of Title X, so that more women and men can receive services that help them consider and achieve both their short-term and long-term family planning needs." The ruling could block about $60 million dollars in family planning funding to Planned Parenthood; the largest abortion provider in the United States. (Berry, 2019) The ruling reinstates President Ronald Reagan's "Protect Life Rule". That rule disallowed the co-location of family planning clinics with those that provide abortions.

The ruling is hailed as another positive step for the Pro-Life advocates. The Pro-Choice movement immediately claimed it is discriminatory and is destined to harm and inconvenience the poorer women in society. The rule further clarified that consistent with statutory requirements, no funds may be extended where abortion is a method of family planning.

The ruling reinforced the fact that no funds are cut from family planning and that federally qualified health centers outnumber abortion centers 20 to 1.

The abortion debate is in full swing with the possibility that Roe v. Wade may make its way to the Supreme Court again. The Court now has the potential to overturn the ruling with the appointment of two recent constitutional justices. At least ten states have passed what is known at "heartbeat bills" that restrict abortion as soon as the fetal heartbeat is detected. The opposite track has been the legislation from New York, Virginia and Vermont mentioned earlier. New Mexico, Maryland and Rhode Island are also supporting bills permitting abortion up to the time of birth. The Title X ruling will likely see more states responding similarly with legislation either restricting abortion or liberalizing it depending upon their political persuasion.

The Daily Wire carried a story on 22 February 2019 about an Idaho couple suing Planned Parenthood for deceptive counseling when the medicated abortion therapy (abortion pill) failed and the wife gave birth to an unwanted third child. ((Bois, 2019). The Christian Post had an article the day before the Title X announcement on Amanda Palmer. (Barnhart, 2019)

Palmer is a 42-year-old musician and supporter of Planned Parenthood and abortion. She has had three abortions herself. The irony the CP article noted was that Palmer wrote a song to her friend "Jill" offering to hold a baby abortion shower. The song Palmer penned more aptly describes the emotional wreck that is often experienced by the woman after an abortion. The lyrics are printed in the article and worth the read if there is any doubt about the emotional burden that some carry after an abortion.

RELIGION & POLITICS
AND THE WORD

And the Word Says

Many theories may exist as to a Christian's responsibility to government. In the United States it was taken by our Forefathers in drafting the originating documents to form this new country that the church and the state should be separate. Over time, the most historical accounting for what this meant is that each had their own sphere of influence in society and thus should be able to conduct their affairs solely, if not only, in their respective place of authority and respect. The current status is somewhat convoluted from the historians' interpretation. Over time, this separation has been used to eliminate religion from any civil activity that government money has been used to support. Prayer and public schools, prayer and high school sports and the Ten Commandments in a courthouse.

A review of Matthew 22:21 is most often quoted respecting the relationship between God and government. By Matthew's account, Jesus was being questioned by some Pharisees and Herodians in a clear effort to entrap Him. Luke 20:20-26 simply refers to His questioners as spies sent by the teachers and chief priests. Their question as recorded by Matthew and in Mark 12:13-17 was whether Jews should pay taxes to the Roman authorities. Jesus's response left them marveling at the answer according to Matthew 22:22. Jesus's answer, after looking at a coin with the image of a Roman leader on it, was "Render unto Caesar the things that are Caesar's, and unto God the things that are God's." It is also noted that Jesus called his questioners "hypocrites" as He was asking for a coin to observe.

This piece of scripture has been debated by some religions as to the necessity to pay taxes such as the case of Quakers refusing to pay a tax to support war. The paying of general taxes was acceptable on the basis that if one enjoys the benefits of government, then supporting the costs of those benefits was necessary. Paul in Corinthians stated that governments are ordained by God and deserve respect. Romans 13:1 is often cited as God's connection to government. The separation of religion and state and the payment of taxes where early debates that continue today though the involvement of religion into political dialog has grown immensely thereafter.

The Relationship

The 2016 United States presidential election was a crystal-clear picture of religion in politics. The last time in American politics that religion was seriously discussed was the election of John F. Kennedy. Kennedy was a Catholic and that fact emerged as a political tool against him, particularly in Protestant strongholds such as the South. Religion only barely made the political landscape in the recent primaries where a prominent Mormon, Mitt Romney, ran.

Supposedly, according to polling, evangelicals strongly endorsed President Donald Trump even though the recognized leaders of evangelicals were split over their endorsements. (Miller, 2018). Eric Miller in an interview with Paul A. Djupe, associate professor of political science at Denison University, quotes Djupe as saying that 81% of identifying evangelicals voted for Trump. He suggests that they arrived at a decision to support Trump for a variety of individual reasons and not because they were unified as being an evangelical. He reasons that political evangelicals are united while religious evangelicals are not. The prognosticators predict that white evangelicals will continue to support conservative values based on self-sufficiency, hard work, lower government debt and less government intrusion into their lives. This block of voters will remain an important group determining elections. Whether it is their convictions of religion or their convictions to a political party that remains uncertain over time.

The interest in religion's impact on the political sphere has brought philosophy into the question. The Internet Encyclopedia of Philosophy, a peer reviewed publication, has devoted a lengthy article on the subject. (Callaway, 2019). The article surveys some of the various ways religion and politics intersect. It is noted early that minorities are often more thought of as to their religious leanings than to their ethnicity. The article breaches the subject of separation of church and state as well as the role of religion in political debate. In the middle, the article explores other derivatives such as liberalization and coercion of religious beliefs.

The U. S. Political Religious Landscape

The U. S. Congressional landscape changed between the 2016 election and the 2018 election. According to Pew Research, the Congress was 94.9% Christion in the 87th Congress of 1961-1962. By the 115th Congress of 2016 that percentage had declined to 90.7%. After the 2018 election, that percentage had declined to 88%. Of the 293 Republicans in the 115th Congress, all but two identified as Christian. Of the 242 Democrats, there were 28 Jews, three Buddhists, three Hindus, two Muslims and one Unitarian Universalist and one unaffiliated. The ten members who declined to state religious affiliation were also Democrats. Protestants continued to decline from 75% to 56% between 1961 and 2016 while Catholics rose from 19% to 31%.

The 116th Congress of 2018 saw the addition of four more of the Jewish faith, one additional Muslim and one more Unitarian Universalist. Eighteen members, all Democrats, declined to declare religious affiliation. Senator Kyrsten Sinema, D-Ariz., stated as being unaffiliated and Rep. Jared Huffman, D-Calif., declared himself as "humanist" and not sure God exists. The landscape of the U. S. Congress is shifting each election gradually though still nine in ten members identify as Christian. On the number side, the 116th Congress had 14 fewer Christians than the 115th and twenty fewer that the 114th Congress. (Sandstrom, 2017).

The changing Congress has five fewer Catholics and three fewer Mormons while the Orthodox Christian group held at five through both elections. The Jewish membership grew by four. The Jewish affiliates represent 6% of Congress while only 2% of the general public claim Jewish. The Muslim membership grew from two to three. Party affiliation is also changing within the Catholic affiliates. In the 114th Congress, Catholics were almost evenly split between Republicans and Democrats (69-68). In the 116th, 87 Catholic members are Democrats and 54 are Republicans. Of the freshmen members of the new Congress, 49% align with Protestant and 30% with Catholic. The new Congress has the lowest number of Christians and Protestants of the last eleven Congresses that data were collected. (Faith on the Hill, 2019).

The alignment of Congress by religious affiliation is establishing a trend that's over two decades long. The change is noticeable with attempts in the new Congress to remove "In God we trust" from the official swearing in script. Also, the new Congress seems more anti-Semitic than previous ones with the new Muslim members being very vocal anti-Semitists.

Congress must show leadership and do so with an abundance of dialog and counsel as Proverbs 11:14 ESV emphasizes: "Where there is no guidance, a people falls, but in an abundance of counselors there is safety." One can hope that even as the religious profile of the American Congress changes that there remains an abundance of counselors focused on God's path. Mark 3:24 ESV gives this sage observation about the divisiveness that the changing profile might likely create: "If a kingdom is divided against itself, that kingdom cannot stand." Psalm 33:12 ESV should be engraved in every corner of the congressional buildings as a reminder that the founding fathers embedded Christianity into virtually every fabric of American governance for a reason. It reads: "Blessed is the nation whose God is the Lord, the people whom he has chosen as his heritage!"

The wise worded book of Proverbs forewarns of the outcome of both righteous and wicked rule in chapter 29:2 ESV which reads: "When the righteous increase, the people rejoice, but when the wicked rule, the people groan." Let us hope that the governance of this country remains righteous and as in Proverbs 11, continues to seek the counsel of those who can advise on righteous governance according to God's directives.

Romans 13:1 ESV is often cited as to our allegiance to government. It is a reminder that government, good or bad in our minds, is given its authority by God. Since we do not know of God's longer-term plan, the bad must be tolerated along with the good. By faith, we must trust that God's plan is not without reason. The verse in Romans reads: "Let every person be subject to the governing authorities. For there is no authority except from God, and those that exist have been instituted by God." "Being instituted by God" is key to understanding that what is, is not without design and purpose. Daniel 2:20-21 lays down the ultimatum as well as the reminder that everyone is leadership is there by the grace of God and they can become history by the same authority. "Daniel answered and said: "Blessed be the name of God forever and ever, to whom belong wisdom and might. He changes times and seasons; he removes kings and sets up kings; he gives wisdom to the wise and knowledge to those who have understanding.""

A Complex Situation

Michele Margolis, an assistant professor of political science at the University of Pennsylvania, poses a new conundrum in her new book "From Politics to the Pews," She suggests that politics quite often influences our decision as to which church or denomination we choose to affiliate. The normal reasoning has been our deeply held beliefs lead us to a political affiliation rather than the reverse which she proposes. Margolis was interviewed by Kelsey Dallas of the Deseret News. The article continues with the statistic that the rise in non-affiliation was polled at being 12% of the population in 1996 and is now 25% in 2016. (Dallas, 2018). For decades, scholars thought that the relationship of religion and politics was a one-way street. Religion governed our political leanings. Margolis does bring up some valid points about our life experience influencing our position on a particular subject. Every congregation has experienced the ebb and flow Margolis cites when members attend church, disappear for a while, may reattend or may never return. Life's influence often forces people's departure from organized religion. It's not religion's fault and it's not that religion often remains critically important to the non-attending member. It is at this time in life for many that their interest in politics may peak. Often it seems that a person's choice of a political group may be the reason they return as faithful church goers and believers or not. It is as though that at this mature adult stage it is what is happening now that supplants the longer-term philosophical view of life. That is, politics is more influential than religion. The Pew Research Center reported that 1 in 10 people who chose a different congregation or church was because of the unit's religious teachings or political stances. We can see this clearly by declining or increasing memberships in mainstream denominations. There are religious worship alternatives that more closely align with a person's political vision and these are the places congregationally dissatisfied members migrate.

2016 Election

The 2016 election brought the voting power of evangelical Christians to the forefront. Pew Research and the Brookings Survey were reporting a sizable lead by Hillary Clinton over Donald Trump as late as October 2016. Voters identifying as Democrat were 95% behind Clinton while only 87% of identified Republicans has committed to Trump. It was at this late point in the election that white evangelicals in particular became noticed. Nearly seven out of ten were firmly voting Trump. Fifteen percent were not committed, and fifteen percent indicated they were voting Clinton. Protestants were firmly behind Trump while white Catholics were evenly split between the two candidates. The Catholic population in general favored Clinton 57% to 33%. Religiously unaffiliated leaned heavily towards Clinton, 69% to 17%. (Robert P. Jones, 2016).

Trump, and likely Clinton as well, were not the most individually moral persons by many standards. The question arose why white evangelicals along with a good majority of Americans were willing to let personal morality issues take the background over political choices. It seems that Americans were transitioning from thinking personal moral character was a necessity in holding a public office. The poll results on this question in 2016 found that 70% of Republicans, 61% of Democrats and 63% of Independents said that public officials can behave ethically in their professional roles even if they acted immorally in their personal life. This fact has played out subsequently in that many public figures have been called on their personal behavior but still retain their public office or public stature. This polling question was also asked in 2011 and the biggest shift in the positive was among white evangelicals. The jump from 2011 to 2016 was a 42% bump among white evangelicals. There was also a 26% decline among all Americans that thought a religious belief was an important attribute for a candidate.

We know how the election turned out with Trump winning the Presidency by essentially carrying everything except the two coasts. Clinton won the majority of popular votes thanks to the big coastline cities but lost the electoral college vote. The 2016 election results began a serious study of evangelical influence in elections and particularly the showing of white evangelicals.

Every Landscape was Changing

Not only were evangelicals changing the election landscape, they were also changing the makeup of the American Christian community. Over the last short period of time, it's reported that half of all Americans have looked for a new congregation. (Choosing a New Church or House of Worship, 2016). Just like political candidates, the church has to offer something enticing to keep adherents. It's obvious that moving residences requires seeking a new church. There is more to the story than the obvious though. Marriage, divorce and disagreements with clergy or members ranked remarkably low as a reason. The "something" in the middle was revealed to be problems with the church or changes in their personal beliefs.

Roughly 45% of Americans who have lived in a community less than five years have gone church shopping. Around 20% of those living a community for more than five years have sought out another congregation. A main driver for church shopping according to the survey is the quality of sermons, 83%. The quality of Christian education for their children scored 56%.

These results led to the question as to what "quality of sermons" meant. It seems the leading determination of quality was preaching the Bible, conservative Christian values and positive on civil rights. As at this writing, the United Methodist Church (UMC) is in St. Louis debating whether to keep its present directive on clergy and teaching or becoming more liberalized. Since this is a global meeting for them and there are more conservative countries than the United States, the assumption is that they will vote to keep their current directive of conservative Biblical teaching and guidelines. It was voted 438 to 384 on 26 February 2019 to keep to its "Traditional Plan" which is against same-sex marriage and non-celibate gay clergy. By the narrow margin in the vote, you can expect the liberal arm of the denomination will push to have this issue on the docket at future conventions. It was the strength of the African delegation that won the vote. Observers say that if only the North American contingent was counted, the UMC would now be liberal. (Steele, 2019)

We have witnessed the demise of some denominations and the core item for their membership decline seems to stem from their more liberal, less Biblical standards. The Pew research seems to indicate that church members are not the least bit hesitant in moving membership. There is clearly a group of Christians that though forgiving on the political front, they are less forgiving about compromised Biblical teaching. "While conservative churches aren't growing as quickly as they once were, mainline churches are on a path toward extinction. The mainline churches are finding that as they move further away from Biblical Christianity, the closer they get to their inevitable demise." (Carter, 2015). Additionally, the use of percentages to tell the story of church membership is misleading. Some denominations are losing people while other non-mainline churches are increasing in memberships. Also, the actual number of people that say they are Christian continues to increase. So, in real numbers, Christianity in the United States is still growing. Because the population is also growing and much of that growth is by people of other faiths or no affiliation, the percentage declines.

A New Generation

With the political and church congregational profile changing, it is wise to gain a better understanding of the upcoming generation. The next in line to be leaders both politically and congregational is the millennials. They are those born 1982 to 2002. They also have been penned with a rather unique name of mosaics. We'll see how both names are appropriate.

Here forward they shall be referred to as mosaics. They have one unique interest that was not an overly high priority of their predecessors. Mosaics are family people. They rate very highly their relationship with their family. They have lived through a rather peaceful time in America. Wars have not stirred the emotions like it did with the boomers nor have there really been a lot of domestic disturbances to interrupt their lives. Family relations could be classified as being tight and they are not "ashamed" to be seen with their parents in public.

Mosaics are fluid with their friendships. Boomers still have friends from their high school days or military days. Mosaic have close friends but change friends often. They are noted for being sensitive about their relationships and try hard not to disrupt the dynamics of groups. They are strongly committed to educational attainment. They grew up when having a college education was the most highly taunted avenue to a successful high middle American income. Parents sacrificed for their education, the school system was redesigned to help them get into college and the colleges and universities created brand new courses just for them.

Mosaics have been the most positive generation. Family incomes generally rose during their developmental years, the U. S. economy was steady, and opportunities seemed plentiful. They are tolerant of differences and are experientially oriented. They are very trusting in institutions. You can see mosaic characteristics clearly in the U. S. Congress as younger members get elected as was the case in the 2018 election. They wish to change things seeing only the future as being no different than their past which was mostly uneventful and little to fear.

They are believers with 96% believing in God and 65% believe in the Bible. The concern is that their interpretation and conviction to the words of the Bible are weak. Only 44% believe that Jesus was resurrected and 53% believe that Jesus sinned while on earth. A startling two-thirds believe that salvation does not depend on Jesus. Only a third think they will continue attending church once totally on their own. The older group of this generation have already made that decision and church membership is reflective of this. Mosaics demand a solid foundation of church teachings. They come to church to make sense of the contemporary world. They want a message that is applicable to them and not some esoteric piece of philosophy. What they do bring forth is perhaps a movement back to the traditional Biblical teachings that prevailed in every Christian church. There will and need to be change. Since this generation is not linear in thinking the new church messages will have to be intuitive, personal, authentic to the Word and solid. For mosaics, the worst is seeing the church with a different personality every time they attend. This is not what they are looking for in a church or a political party. (Oppel, 2007).

Was Christianity Meant to Change with the Times

Megachurches have less defined firm doctrines, denominations are accepting gay marriages, the Pope is for open borders everywhere and the teachings of Heaven and Hell are some state of mind rather than an eternal existence. Public opinion is also weak on conviction. Over a third of polled respondents believe Jesus will never return, about a third do not believe in the literal translation of the Bible and two-thirds think there are alternative ways to an eternal life other than the single route the Bible describes.

The historic route of Christianity and its church differ greatly from the church descriptions in the Bible. As the Apostles disappeared, their teachings were left open to alterations by degrees. The Romans between A. D. 313 and A. D. 380 probably solidified the potential for Christianity to be the world's largest religious group. It was in A. D. 380 that Emperor Theodosius I declared it the official state religion. It's growth thereafter seemed to be one of assimilating other religions including paganism into their fold rather than conquering or dominating.

The Apostle Paul was a truest. His teachings followed those of Jesus. He gave many warnings to the church about falling away from the Word and its sound doctrines. He apparently foresaw that the church as Jesus intended could be blended with other religious ideas and not be a strong adherent to the gospel. Peter too warned that even Paul's writings could be twisted into new meanings. John warned about the deceptions that might sway the church and Jude wrote almost beggingly for the church to earnestly defend the faith. Christianity was not intended to evolve. These leaders in the formation of the church of Jesus clearly argued against changes. The Bible states nothing should be added or taken away from the Word. (Jones, 2015).

Is It Religion, Politics or Secularism

It seems appropriate to look at this statement by Peter Beinart in the April, 2017 edition of *The Atlantic:* "Some observers predicted that this new secularism would ease cultural conflict, as the country settled into a near-consensus on issues such as gay marriage. After Barack Obama took office, a Center for American Progress report declared that "demographic change," led by secular, tolerant young people, was "undermining the culture wars." In 2015, the conservative writer David Brooks, noting Americans' growing detachment from religious institutions, urged social conservatives to "put aside a culture war that has alienated large parts of three generations."

That was naive. Secularism is indeed correlated with greater tolerance of gay marriage and pot legalization. But it's also making America's partisan clashes more brutal. And it has contributed to the rise of both Donald Trump and the so-called alt-right movement, whose members see themselves as proponents of white nationalism. As Americans have left organized religion, they haven't stopped viewing politics as a struggle between "us" and "them." Many have come to define *us* and *them* in even more primal and irreconcilable ways." (Beinart, 2017).

This is a good summation of the battle that brought religion into the mainstream political movement. Interestingly, it also revived the cultural issue by reintroducing terms like white nationalism, alt-left, alt-right and neo-Nazism. Along with these words Americans were learning words like homophobic, misogamist, Islamophobia, and LGBTTQQIAAP. It cannot be said that Americans are abandoning religion and becoming more "us" and "them". The Christian population as stated elsewhere is growing in whole numbers, but people are leaving mainline denominations for alternatives. If we look closely at the changing dynamics of church goers, statistics indicate that they are abandoning liberalized churches and returning to the conservative teaching Biblical ones. It could be the migration to churches that teach the Word as it was meant has led to a body of church goers that are less willing to submit to liberalizing everything; especially their beliefs.

This may be secularism's return. A younger generation, particularly the mosaics addressed earlier, are very accepting of individualism. Beinart is right in one sense. Our debates are more primal and perhaps at the point of being irreconcilable. The sides seem to be moving so far apart that a middle ground no longer exists. So, politics and religion are now synonymous.

Another take comes from Julie Butters of Boston College. (Butters, 2019). In her article she quotes Bruce J. Schulman, Professor of History. Her writing and his quotes present this scenario: "Opposition to the secularism of the '60s, to abortion, and to measures that established a clearer separation between church and state, such as the banning of school-sponsored prayer, galvanized the Religious Right. Evangelicals would boost the campaigns of Republicans like Ronald Reagan, George H. W. Bush (Hon.'89), and George W. Bush. Now, "the role of evangelical Protestants is so strong," says Schulman, that it shapes "the entire presidential selection process." (Schulman, 2019).

Today, most Americans want a president of faith. In a 2014 Pew Research Center survey, 53 percent of Americans said they would be less likely to support a presidential candidate who does not believe in God. As recent elections have shown, they also expect presidential candidates to talk about their personal faith. (Butters, 2019).

"The rise of the Religious Right has changed the landscape so that" in most of the United States overt religious expression is an expected part of our politics, says Schulman (Schulman, 2019), "and overt irreligion or non-religion is something that's become more or less unacceptable."

As some see religion as an integral part of picking candidates and eventually electoral victors, the assumption made by Beinart may be foretelling of how our future political battles will be framed. The following list of religion and governmental association found in the Bible is from Christians in Politics, a United Kingdom organization:

"From the creation mandate in Genesis we received a cultural mandate – to develop institutions upon the earth. In this task, we understand that our relational priorities are governed by the fact that we are all endowed with equal worth and dignity. In other words, there are no premier league people. Under God's authority, this essential equality is the starting point for all human government. Being made in the image of God, we are called to faithfully manifest that image in our day to day work. We govern because he governs. Throughout the rest of the Bible God keeps calling people back to this task. With Joseph we see how God uses his anointed to govern in an alien land for the protection and prosperity of his people. Genesis also shows that emancipation from oppression is on God's agenda.

In Exodus we see how Moses was a deeply political figure, and we begin to receive the laws that express God's heart for good government.

With a strong emphasis upon personal and corporate morality, and caring for the poor, Leviticus shows us how the law is designed to cover all the dimensions of Israel's relations with God, with one another and with the earth.

Numbers proposes a democratic process under God with the selection of representative leaders.

Deuteronomy affirms the idea of equality under the law for Kings and subjects alike.

Joshua shows the need for integrity of leadership, and a strong national identity in which morality is required as a distinctive for God's people.

Judges shows how the Lord raises up and empowers people to lead the nation out of sin, error and judgment. It also shows the need for women to assume national leadership responsibilities.

Ruth shows how social responsibility transcends legal contract.

Samuel 1 & 2 reaffirm equality under the law.

The books of 1 & 2 Kings chart the good, the bad and the ugly of how to govern. These books show how leaders are subject to greater accountability for their actions.

The books of 1 & 2 Chronicles show the Lord's heart for government through the reply to Solomon's request for wisdom to govern, and they place the responsibility for national renewal with God's people.

Ezra demonstrates the power of the Word to restore identity and direction to a people.

Nehemiah teaches how we learn about how the restoration of authority.

Esther and Mordecai were raised up to lobby the authorities to save their people.

Job teaches us about trusting a sovereign God in trials.

The Psalms cover the whole range of effects that the human condition and the righteousness of God.

Proverbs was written to instruct princes how to govern when they become kings.

Ecclesiastes talks about the wisdom needed to rule.

Song of Solomon describes our relational priorities.

Isaiah describes the coming saviour and his Kingdom – the increase of whose government there shall be no end.

Jeremiah illustrates the need to speak truth to power.

Lamentations shows how God can use one nation to punish another.

Ezekiel describes how the river from the temple heals the nations.

Daniel demonstrates that God's people can be called to rule in alien, pagan cultures. With an implicit recognition that for engagement in politics there is a time to defy and a time to comply for the people of God. With Daniel we see how integrity is tied to identity, and how the role of the prophetic is important for governmental power. Importantly, the book shows that God's dominion covers all kingdoms, all empires and the whole earth – and that ultimately, all kingdoms will pass into God's own kingdom of love and righteousness.

Hosea attacks hedonism and the abuse of wealth.

Joel challenges public consciousness.

Amos exposes hypocritical rulers.

Obadiah affirms that justice cannot be escaped.

Jonah speaks of responsibility beyond the borders of our own race and ethnicity.

Micah emphasizes the importance of morality, integrity and justice.

Nahum explains how freedom can bring both curses and blessings to a nation.

Habakkuk talks of God's care for the poor.

Zephaniah binds belief with action and demands clear identity.

Haggai re-orders our social priorities in light of God's holiness.

Zechariah reaffirms the absolute authority of God.

… and Malachi warns against complacency and idolatry in national life.

The New Testament

Matthew, Mark, Luke & John cite the governing supremacy of Christ through his statement that 'All authority in heaven and on earth is given unto me' (Matt 28: 18); and when Jesus told Pilate that 'You would have no power over me unless it had been given you from above' (John 9:11).

Acts demonstrates a unified and equal community that is governed by council, consensus and majority; illustrates the need to speak truth to power; and proposes new forms of citizenship. It also shows illustrates the need for religious freedom.

Romans shows the value of secular government; and critiques the human effects of state sanctioned idolatry. Crucially, in stating that that the political authority 'is God's servant for your good (13: 1-4) Paul affirms that political authority comes from God for our benefit.

---

1 Corinthians & 2 Corinthians in identifying the flawed wisdom of hollow philosophies establishes the need for moral reference beyond human ideologies; calls believers to model new, subversive forms of community; outlines the ministry of reconciliation; and values suffering for what is right.

Galatians explains the radical, totalizing freedom given by Christ – that the gospel both necessitates, requires and sustains freedom.

Ephesians describes human responsibility in the spiritual battle that informs earthly authority, and states how the church is to communicate 'the manifold wisdom of God to the rulers and authorities in the heavenly realms'. Demonstrating the good governance of the Kingdom is proposed.

Philippians encourages humility and hope in the face of suffering; and challenges abuses related to social status.

Colossians affirms the supremacy of Christ in human affairs by stating that 'Thrones or dominions or authorities – all things were created through him and for him … and in him all things hold together' (1: 16-17); and calls for intellectual rigor to challenge hollow philosophies and human traditions.

---

1 & 2 Thessalonians confirms the value and dignity of labor; and asserts the necessity for the rule of law.

---

1 & 2 Timothy compels believers to pray for government 'first of all' – as a priority for the gospel; values the council of elderly people and encourages young people to lead; explains the role of charity; warns against the corruption that wealth can bring; describes a godless society.

Titus discusses authority amongst diverse social groups.

Philemon deals with slavery and labor.

Hebrews confirms the equality of all people before God, and how justice is indivisible from mercy.

James explains how deeds must accompany words; that favoritism is forbidden in leadership; that a focus upon developing good language and communication is essential for leadership; and how the wisdom that comes from God differs in substance and impact from earthly wisdom.

---

1 Peter calls for believers to 'Be subject for the Lord's sake to every human institution, whether it be the emperor … or to governors.' (2: 13), confirming that all authority is ordained by God, and that submission is required even during persecution. It also shows that the gospel itself has its place in political power by revealing that Jesus 'has gone into heaven and

is at God's right hand—with angels, authorities and powers in submission to him.' (3: 22).

---

2 Peter asserts the value of a clear conscience and good teaching for leadership; and the need to respond to evil with good.

1, 2 & 3 John describes the institutional nature of sin; and the need to provide good role models for leadership.

Jude attacks bad role models for leadership; and shows how when abused, authority can be abdicated.

Revelation affirms the dominion of the kingdom of God above earthly empires; calls Christians to lead as well as serve; condemns those who have put their faith in money and power; and promises a conclusion in which justice is inescapable. It shows how redemption in Jesus Christ is not limited to any one area of the creation. Not only persons, but nations, kingdoms, the entire creation will be reconciled. (Politics in the Bible, 2019).

YOUR VOCATION AND THE WORD

Religion and Your Job

In January, Vice President Mike Pence's wife, Karen, was criticized for returning to teaching at a Christian school she had taught at before. The criticism was centered around the school's principle of marriage being between a man and woman. The Vice President also mentioned this situation at his presentation to the Conservative Political Action Conference February 28, 2019. Karen Pence's decision to return to teaching at a school where she had taught before should seem an unlikely national news story. Yet the New York Times chose to make a monumental announcement about it. (Haag, 2019). Mrs. Pence had taught art at this school between 2001 and 2013 but because it requires its employees to refrain from engaging in moral misconduct her returning was somewhat abhorrent. Her employment at a private religious school where she had taught when her husband was a Congressman and from which her daughter graduated quickly devolved into politics. The media and the anti-Trump crowd quickly tied her place of employment into aligning with the current U. S. administration. All of which demonstrates that even you are not allowed to have a job of your choosing and perhaps historic connection unless the social justice promoters approve.

The very first part of Genesis describes God at work creating His kingdom. He assigned Adam and Eve to work His garden and gave them dominion over His creation so that it would grow. If God created work and then stated that it was good, He rightfully ordained work to be good. Work well done gives us pleasure and work done for others pleases God, James

1:17. The Bible also condemns those able to work and don't, Proverbs 10:4; 2 Thessalonians 3:10-12.

Some Scripture relating to work:

- Everyone should work if they're able to. — "For even when we were with you, we gave you this rule: 'The one who is unwilling to work shall not eat.'" 2 Thessalonians 3:10
- Work for God's glory and not for personal motivations of money, power or fame. — "...whatever you do, do it for the glory of God." 1 Corinthians 10:31
- Work with all your heart. — "Whatever you do, work at it with all of your heart, as working for the Lord, not for human masters." Colossians 3:23
- Pray for wisdom and God's guidance regarding decisions related to your work. — "If any of you lacks wisdom, you should ask God, who gives generously to all without finding fault, and it will be given to you." James 1:5 (also see Joshua 9:1-27 which describes the consequences when Joshua and the Israelites failed to consult the Lord and were deceived by the Gibeonites)
- Pray for the Holy Spirit to produce spiritual fruit in you in the way you go about your work. — "The fruit of the Spirit is love, joy, peace, patience, kindness, goodness, faithfulness, gentleness and self-control." Galatians 5:22-23
- Think of your work as an expression of love for God and people. — When asked by one of the teachers of the law which is the most important commandment, Jesus replied: "The most important one is this: 'Hear, O Israel: The Lord our God, the Lord is one. Love the Lord your God with all your heart and with all your soul and with all your mind and with all your strength.' The second is this: 'Love your neighbor as yourself.' There is no commandment greater than these." Mark 12:29-31
- Pray for God's favor and blessing on your work. — "Don't worry about anything; instead, pray about everything. Tell God what you need and thank him for all he has done. Then you will experience God's peace, which exceeds anything we can understand. His

peace will guard your hearts and minds as you live in Christ Jesus."
Philippians 4:6-7
- Set aside the Sabbath to rest from your work. — "Remember the Sabbath day by keeping it holy. Six days you shall labor and do all your work, but the seventh day is a sabbath to the Lord your God. On it you shall not do any work... For in six days the Lord made the heavens and the earth, the sea, and all that is in them, but he rested on the seventh day. Therefore, the Lord blessed the Sabbath day and made it holy." Exodus 20:8-11 (Stallard, 2019).

Perhaps the Times should have consulted Colossians 3:23 ESV "Whatever you do, work heartily, as for the Lord and not for men." Jon Bloom writing for desiringGod.org put it this way: "...your calling today in whatever God has given you to do: *make God look great*. According to 1 Corinthians 7:17–24, your job (assuming it's not inherently unethical or immoral) is a ministry assignment from God. It may not be your career assignment, but it's today's assignment. And God wants you to carry out that assignment with dependent faith, diligence, and excellence." The omission is any mention that your job has to have approval from society nor should your job be judged by secular rules. (Bloom, 2015).

The Bible instructs us to the salt and the light in this world. That means even in our work. The first step is to have a relationship with God through Jesus. The Bible does not give us a roadmap of what career or employment to have. The freedom of willpower drives that decision, but that decision is always correct for us if our relationship with Christ is increasingly intimate. God has gifted us with certain talents. As we become more aware of these gifts, they lead us toward vocations that seem more natural for our talents. Understanding what gifts a person has is challenging for young people but if they stay the course with Jesus, the gifts will become apparent.

A discussion of our angels hearing our every word and communicating that to God sets in motion our future. Hebrews 1:14 says, "Are not all angels ministering spirits sent to serve those who will inherit salvation?" Believing and experiencing Jesus in your life enables the angels to help with career choices. Angels are God's creation and were probably part of God's creation before His third day of creation. They are not always recognizable as Hebrews 13:2 says, "Do not forget to entertain strangers, for by so doing some people have entertained angels without knowing it." For those looking for a God guided vocation, there may be many angels who are unrecognizable as such helping with the decision. People have to believe that they are where they are in life's journey by their faith. God gives to those that ask. Ask the right questions. Angels have many duties: Angels carry out God's judgment; Angels serve God; Angels praise God; Angels are messengers; Angels protect God's people; Angels do not marry; Angels do not die; Angels encourage people. (Gliddon, 2002).

Everyone Has an Opinion

To garner an idea of how strongly some people hold that Christian beliefs should be totally absent in the workforce, some commentary on the reaction of Karen Pence returning to her previous teaching position is provided. It wasn't her return to teaching that set the rampage off, it was where she chose to work. To offset the sampling of negativism, some supporting opinions are also provided.

The first and perhaps the most egregious if not pejorative is the following from The Daily Beast. "That Karen Pence would be willing to teach at such an institution (that also insists that marriage stands for "the uniting of one man and one woman") is no surprise. She already did, at this school specifically, for 12 years."

"The Pence's' religious beliefs regarding the unacceptable nature of LGBTQ identity, proscriptive and subordinate roles for women, and rigid understandings of the relationship between sex and gender—all reflected in the policies and practices of Immanuel Christian School— are widely known." (Byard, 2019). The title Ms. Byard's article sets the tone by declaring that Mrs. Pence should not be teaching at this school, period. "And that is the source of the deep consternation and distress at her decision", Ms. Byard continues. Consternation and distress because there exist an institution and a teacher that does not buy into the anti-Christian philosophy.

The Daily Caller called out the liberal bashing of Mrs. Pence's choice of employment. "Some seized on these principles to accuse both the school and the second lady of bigotry. The Pence's never seem to miss an opportunity to show their public service only extends to some," the Human Rights Campaign said." The complaining continued: "Former White House aide and current CNN commentator Keith Boykin called Trump-supporting gay people "self-hating," in response to Karen Pence's new job." The Daily Caller, a conservative news source, had to simply state the obvious in closing: "The Pence's are devout evangelical Christians and are frequently derided in some left-wing circles for their faith." (Davis, 2019)

The BuzzFeed News began with this title to an article: "Karen Pence Is Teaching at A Christian School That Bans LGBT Students and Employees". (Hall, 2019). Some fact checking would have clarified that the school does not ban LGBT students nor employees. They welcome any that wish to attend or work there but acknowledge that their adherence to Biblical teachings might make those who do not feel uncomfortable around a group of students and employees that do. What Ms. Hall fails to consider is that Mrs. Pence is not an employee of the Federal Government nor is she an elected official. Thus Mrs. Pence is free to choose her employment as she sees fit. The fact that BuzzFeed let the headline stand, though erroneous, was sufficient for them to make their point to those that read the liberal news feed.

David French of the National Review was quick to catch on to the attention Mrs. Pence's employment decision was attracting from the liberal left: "On the intolerant critics of the second lady, Karen Pence is a believing Christian woman. She took a part-time job at a private Christian school. And this, believe it or not, is a scandal. Don't believe me? Her job has already merited not just one, but two critical *Washington Post* stories. There's the obligatory CNN report, accompanied by a piece of commentary that argues the school is "like a real-life setting for 'The Handmaid's Tale.'" Sounds terrible. Has she joined a fringe Christian cult? Have the Branch

Davidians descended on Northern Virginia? Are teachers kept in a form of sex slavery to produce children for the principal? Let's let the *New York Times* set the lurid scene:

"Karen Pence, the second lady of the United States, returned to teaching art this week, accepting a part-time position at a private Christian school that does not allow gay students and requires employees to affirm that marriage should only be between a man and a woman."

Hmm, something doesn't seem right. I've been involved in Christian education for much of my life. I attended a Christian college, my oldest kids attended a dozen consecutive years of Christian schooling, I served a term as chairman of their school's board, and I've represented Christian institutions for more than two decades, and I've never once seen a Christian institution declare that no gays are allowed.''" (French, 2019).

It seems Mr. French has a better take on the theme behind all of the consternation of the Second Lady returning to work and that is "intolerance". The liberal movement cannot accept that someone can be a Christian and live by Christian standards with the same liberty that many choose to not live by. Intolerance of any expression of Biblical faith is threatening to the progressive movement. In this instance, the LGBQ movement rose to arms using whatever pernicious arguments that could. They particularly honed-in on making it seem like not accepting a life practice that you are faithfully against is some sort of attack on the person. Christianity teaches judging the behavior and not the person. More accurately, the Bible instructs Christians to not judge but to rebuke sin and evil. Luke 17:3 uses the word "rebuke" and says further that if the party repents, then forgive them. Too often the "judge not, lest you be judged" is incorrectly applied. There is a difference between judging and being judgmental. The latter is the rebuke. "Many people cite Matthew 7:1 about not judging others, but they never bother to read down to verse 6, where Jesus says, "Do not give what is holy to dogs, and do not throw your pearls before swine...." He was talking about *people* who are dogs and swine! To obey verse 6, you must make some *judgmental* decisions about the person's character!" (Cole, 2005).

The Huffington Post went so far as to claim that Christian schools are a real threat to our academic freedom. Let it be said that academic freedom is the sole preserve of colleges and universities. It is not some legal freedom entrenched in some legislation. It is a practice and a practice only that has been adopted by higher education to allow the freedom of expression so that new ideas are not denied the opportunity to be tested and debated. A K through 12 school has mandated legal standards of achievement. A private K through 12 Christian school can hardly be accused of being a threat to academic freedom since their education mandate is first set by the State and most often the Federal guidelines as well. That is all irrelevant since the Huffington Post's byline is designed to get attention and not express any degree of truth.

The Huffington Post made it a point to introduce bigotry into the discussion since it was a few days behind other articles on this subject and it had to come up with a new angle: "Immanuel Christian is not unusual. Too many religious schools at all levels regulate the personal conduct of their employees and students, restrict the books teachers can assign or students can read, and demand fealty to narrow constructions of religious identity, while enshrining bigotry into their bylaws." (Perry, 2019).

Prejudice and Progressivism

The opinions about Mrs. Pence's choice of employment brings forth two evidential philosophies; prejudice and progressive politics. Prejudice is the tendency to group people into similar categories. Often the grouping is not relevant, and the group may only have one thing in common. It is like saying everyone who likes baseball likes hotdogs. In the political world today, it is Christians that are being grouped into any number of newly named sub-categories such as racist, homophobes, bigots and intolerants. Prejudice can be an outcome of us merely being uncomfortable in a group with which we lack something familiar. It is how prejudice is manifested that is at issue.

Church goers have been classified by some researchers as being very prejudice. The Bible and many of Jesus's teachings encourage accepting of all people and loving your neighbor. These messages are not being prejudice but just the opposite. Christians would generally see prejudice as being sinful but follow the rule of loving the sinner. Prejudice is method of protection. We encapsulate ourselves and exclude others as a way of preserving our self-worth. This is not a necessary action since believers have already been given a great guarantee of eternal life. Perhaps groups who condemn Christians and their choices are fearful that Christians are a threat to them. They may be guilty of prejudice. They may have the insecurity that says that to protect what is familiar and comfortable to them is to condemn and challenge anyone who has a contrary opinion. This discomfort was very evident with Mrs. Pence's choice of employment and religious education in general.

Michael Kruger cites literature in his series called "The Ten Commandments of Progressive Christianity" that liberal Christianity is not Christianity. (Kruger, 2018). Kruger begins with concepts from J. Gresham Machen's 1923 book *Christianity and Liberalism* where Machen's argument is "…that the liberal understanding of Christianity was, in fact, not just a variant version of the faith, nor did it represent simply a different denominational perspective, but was an entirely different religion altogether." Kruger followed with this observation: "What is remarkable about Machen's book was how prescient it was. His description of liberal Christianity–a moralistic, therapeutic version of the faith that values questions over answers and being "good" over being "right"–is still around today in basically the same form." Although political progressiveness is far more encompassing than good versus right, they bring the same approach to their view of conservative Christianity. Progressive Christianity is more about making the person feel good rather the God feeling good about us. The recent debates among certain denominations over liberalism or Biblical teachings are good examples of what Machen addressed almost one hundred years ago.

Using Your Talent

Corinthians tells us that what we do should be for Christ and 1 Peter 4:10 tells us to use our gifts to serve others. What is unrecognized by those that complain about Karen Pence's returning to teach in Christian school is the lives she is touching. For her, I'm sure she is serving Christ and using her artistic talents to serve others. Students may become more inspired to pursue art and others may observe her character and emulate a positive and faithful person. Jesus instructed that we should love the Lord and to love others. (Brown, 2016). "Today's popular culture teaches that the ends justify the means, a message of "I can do whatever I need to in order to get what I want." This is certainly not a new concept. At the end of the book of Judges, we read that "everyone did what was right in his own eyes" (Judg. 17:6)." (Whelchel, 2018). This statement characterizes a generation of thinkers that practice this very philosophy of living and working while condemning another for doing the same thing. Though both are in err about the purpose of their work, it shows the hypocrisy of what they practice.

In Ephesians 2:10, God tells us: "We are His workmanship, created in Christ Jesus for good works, which God prepared beforehand that we should walk in them." John 14:13-14 says: "And whatever you ask in My name, that I will do, that the Father may be glorified in the Son. If you ask anything in My name, I will do it." These passages are all about the talents God has given us and seeking God's guidance in using them to glorify Him. The interesting thing is that if you use your talents for God's purpose, He will give you more. If you spend your time serving others, He will give you more time to do just that. The well never runs dry. You have to question what talents are those that are so quick to criticize and pass judgement using. True also is that by using their talent of being able to put their critical opinions before a reading public, that their well may dry up if their intent is self-serving.

We are guided to use our talents to the fullest. "Whatever your hand finds to do, do it with all your might" (Ecclesiastes 9:10). Matthew 5:10-12 ESV reminds us that in the process of following God's wishes about using our gifts we may encounter the wrath of others but always be always take comfort in these words: "Blessed are those who are persecuted for righteousness' sake, for theirs is the kingdom of heaven. "Blessed are you when others revile you and persecute you and utter all kinds of evil against you falsely on my account. Rejoice and be glad, for your reward is great in heaven, for so they persecuted the prophets who were before you." A good closing to prejudice and progressive politics are these words from Romans 2:6-8 ESV: "He will render to each one according to his works: to those who by patience in well-doing seek for glory and honor and immortality, he will give eternal life; but for those who are self-seeking and do not obey the truth, but obey unrighteousness, there will be wrath and fury."

Hypocrisy

"The Bible calls hypocrisy a sin. There are two forms hypocrisy can take: that of professing belief in something and then acting in a manner contrary to that belief, and that of looking down on others when we ourselves are flawed." (What does the Bible say about hypocrisy?, 2019). Is it not hypocritical for some to condemn the work of others while at the same time doing work that many others might also condemn? The condemnation is not only of the person for choosing to do the work that they have chosen but also their employer. Beyond that, they are also condemning the whole group of like employers. In the case of Mrs. Pence and the Immanuel Christian School, the critics have levied an assortment of opinions about Christian schools to include a judgement on private schools in general. At the same time that they are criticizing they are offering no sound reasoning for such abhorrent objections other than the school and schools do not buy into their LBQT lifestyle. Objection to the LBQT lifestyle is the hypocrisy since correspondingly they refuse to buy into the Christian lifestyle. It is the one-way nature of so many arguments against Christianity that are hypocritical. Recall looking down on others while they too are flawed and professing to belief in freedom of choice while complaining about another's choices.

Jesus on the sermon on the mount spoke about being blinded by your belief. Remove the plank in your own eye so you can see more clearly to remove the speck of sawdust from your neighbor's eye. The slogan of Gay Pride (Week) is an example of being so full of pride that the participants promote an overwhelming degree of self-righteousness since they are so believing that they are right, and all others are wrong. Self-righteousness was certainly on display in the many articles and opinions that proliferated the media after Mrs. Pence returned to her old job. Pride can bring a downfall.

Pride is all about finding fault. It seems to be quite easy for people to find fault in others while skipping the part about self-diagnosis. It is clearly seen that pride has led some to being so superficial that it's hard to take their comments seriously. Their condemnation of Christians is some huge defense mechanism that they have to throw up so that they can continue along their path without the discomfort of confronting their own shortcomings and faults. In today's media you can read how defensive some writers, reporters and institutions are when there is even just a hint that there's resistance to their way of thinking or acting.

Romans 12:16 says we should live in harmony with one another and not be proud but be willing associate with other people. It also says to not be conceited. The definition of conceit is having excessive pride in oneself. Philippians 2:3 brings together both pride and conceit in one verse. "Do nothing out of selfish ambition or vain conceit...". For those who so adamantly oppose Christianity and the values it espouses, they glaringly expose their own self-righteousness, the faulty pride in themselves and the conceit deep in their hearts. The combination of which is the framework for being a hypocrite. Before condemning something that is rather benign such as one's work, they should do a self-examination of their own values. Values that particularly relate to the treatment of other people. No cause is cause to berate an individual.

The Media's Disdain for Christianity

A vocation is a vocation so being a National Football League (NFL) player or coach means your vocation is sports. The disdain for Christianity is very prevalent in sports broadcasting as well. The sports media swooned of Colin Kaepernick taking a knee during the national anthem in protest to racial issues and law enforcement. It became a complete movement within the NFL and sports viewers showed their distaste for political theater in their sports entertainment by tuning out. Viewership and on-field attendance have dropped accordingly. Yet there were several Christian athletes in the NFL that openly showed their faith, but they were put to the side by the media.

This quote from an opinion piece in Liberty Nation sums it up well about Christian athletes for the Philadelphia Eagles upon their 2018 Super Bowl win: "Outspoken Christians in sports are rebels in the eyes of the media. In fact, Christians are rebels anyway. But hasn't it always been like that? Christ was a rebel. He preached grace over damnation. He spoke of love rather than judgment. Most importantly, he fulfilled prophesy. The outspoken Christians for the Eagles speak the same thing. However, there are attempts to silence commentators in the media who speak highly of these men." Two of these Eagle men of faith are Carson Wentz and Nick Foles. Both were stars in the Eagles win over the New England Patriots that day. ESPN even blacked out Clemson Tigers coach Dabo Swinney in 2015, while conducting a postgame interview when he "thanked the good Lord" for the opportunity to compete and coach. ESPN claimed it was some kind of accident. (Dempsey, 2018).

What about interviewing to be a judge in one of the nation's high courts. Even the liberal body of Congress is not shy about contravening the law and inquiring about a person's religious beliefs as if that it is a necessary qualification of being a judge whose job is to judicate a law that these same people perhaps help draft. David Limbaugh of the Spectrum made this observation in a July, 2018 article: "People on the left are outraged when you question their patriotism, their dedication to the nation as founded and their respect for the Constitution as originally written, but they continually vindicate our concerns."

"The most recent example is the left's unhinged mania at Judge Amy Coney Barrett's inclusion on President Trump's list of potential Supreme Court appointees. In times of perceived crisis–and this is certainly one of those times for leftists–they show their colors, and you can color them militantly opposed to Barrett, in large part because of her Catholicism. And guess what else. Rumor is that she frequents a Bible study, as well." (Limbaugh, 2018). Since Judge Amy Coney Barrett's confirmation hearing, nominee Brian Buescher's hearing for appointment to the U. S. District Court of Nebraska was challenged because of his membership in the Knights of Columbus. (O'Reilly, 2018). Obviously, your religious leanings are of grave concern for holding such high positions as a District Court judge or pro-athlete but moving into 2019, it is also of concern for art teachers in a K through 12 school.

America is not alone in battling disdain for Christians. It seems our close neighbor to the North experiences much of what the U. S. endures. In a Bridgehead, (a Canadian publication), article reprinted in Life Site electronic media, writer Jonathon van Maren wrote this: "Canada's progressive politicians have always had an underlying disdain for Christians, but as that disdain becomes more open and part of their legislative agendas, it is rapidly turning into open war. It started with Justin Trudeau's new Governor General Julie Payette mocking people of faith in a speech, comparing those who believe that the universe came about through divine intervention with those who believe in horoscopes. She was promptly defended by (Prime Minister) Justin Trudeau, who was condemned by Conservative leader Andrew Scheer for belittling the beliefs of millions of Canadians. The Canadian commentariat, at least, was almost universally disgusted by her speech, citing it as an example of a figurehead official overstepping her bounds." (Maren, 2017). It is clear that your religious beliefs are factoring into your life outside of your personal domain. The disdain for Christians is not localized but global. The news occasionally reports on Christian persecution in other countries. These may not activate immediate concern but when it becomes personal and impacts your livelihood, it is personal.

SOCIAL JUSTICE AND CHRISTIANITY

Definition

The Federalist papers that were written during the founding of the United States had commentaries on social justice as it was in the 1776 era. Social justice at that time dealt with only one facet and that was the government and citizen economic relationship. The Federalist papers also mentioned that there was no social justice without morality. It has been written in previous chapters that God so blessed us by building into our genetic framework a sense of right and wrong. Previously it mentioned that science has ascertained that this sense of morality exists in infants only months old. Since the rise of the first definition of the term social justice it has expanded to encompass many things beyond government and citizen economic relations. Today, progressives have attached the term to a variety of relationships beyond economics. It is this expansion of the definition that has brought Christianity into the discussion. The following Pachamama Alliance provided this short history of the social justice term:

"Social Justice as a concept arose in the early 19th century during the Industrial Revolution and subsequent civil revolutions throughout Europe, which aimed to create more egalitarian societies and remedy capitalistic exploitation of human labor. Because of the stark stratifications between wealthy and the poor during this time, early social justice advocates focused primarily on capital, property, and the distribution of wealth."

"By the mid-20th century, social justice had expanded from being primarily concerned with economics to include other spheres of social life to include the environment, race, gender, and other causes and manifestations of inequality. Concurrently, the measure of social justice expanded from being measured and enacted only by the nation-state (or government) to include a universal human dimension. For example, governments (still today) measure income inequality among people who share citizenship in common. But social justice can also be considered at the level of humanity as a whole. As the United Nations states: "Slaves, exploited workers and oppressed women are above all victimized human beings whose location matters less than their circumstances." (What is Social Justice?, 2019).

It is the expansion of the social justice tag during the 20th century that brought attention to the environment, race, gender, life choices, politics, reproductive rights and religion. In certain groups religion is seen as barrier to social justice under the expanded definition. The Heritage Foundation applies this analysis of the term: "For its proponents, "social justice" is usually undefined. Originally a Catholic term, first used about 1840 for a new kind of virtue (or habit) necessary for post-agrarian societies, the term has been bent by secular "progressive" thinkers to mean uniform state distribution of society's advantages and disadvantages." (Novak, 2009).

The progressive culture has eliminated the term "equitable" from its vocabulary and suggests that the only thing that is "just" is for everyone to have an "equal" share regardless of their degree of contribution to whatever is being divided or distributed. Estate planning often uses the example of the home farm to distinguish equitable from equal. A couple develop a farm and have children. As the children mature, all but one of the siblings leaves the farm for other work. One of the siblings stays behind and helps Mom and Dad grow and expand the farm. When Mom and Dad pass away, the estate must be settled. If an equal division is sought, those that left the farm get the same from the estate as the one who stayed behind and helped add wealth to the estate. An equitable division would see the sibling that stayed behind and help grow the farm get the lion's share of the estate, perhaps keeping the farm for his or her self and family and the other siblings would get a token share as a reminder of how much their parents loved them as well.

"This definition expresses a whole ideology: that equality is good and ought to be enforced. And note what has happened to the word "equality." In English, equality usually suggests fairness, equity, or the equitable; but what is equitable is often *not* to give people the same portions, but rather to give what is *proportionate* to the efforts of each." (Novak, 2009).

Pope Leo XIII in 1890 recognized the approach of expanded pressure to adopt a broadening adoption of the social justice philosophy. It wrote in one of his letters to churches under his oversight: "It must be first of all recognized that the condition of things inherent in human affairs must be borne with, for it is impossible to reduce civil society to one dead level. Socialists may in that intent do their utmost, but all striving against nature is in vain. There naturally exist among mankind manifold differences of the most important kind; people differ in capacity, skill, health, strength; and unequal fortune is a necessary result of unequal condition." (Leo XIII).

Biblical Justice

The exploitation of the vulnerable is injustice. We are born with an innate sense about right and wrong. The issue today is the expansive definition of justice to include items that may or may not have some moral standing to which a Biblical view of justice would apply.

God imparted to us certain justice principles. These include loving our neighbor, having mercy, showing compassion and simply being respectful to all. Deuteronomy 32:4 tells us that God is justice. He is righteous, holy and just. Psalms 89:14 repeats that God's foundation is righteousness and justice. Following God's way of being just means we should work to make right what is wrong. This is where culture departs ways. What is wrong? What the Biblical world view might consider wrong as in against the teachings of the Bible and what today's culture considers wrong are often miles apart. What the Bible considers right are what some consider wrong. God sent His Son to walk among human kind as an example of justice. The justice component of Jesus's life is not as widely spoken about as some of His other teachings but are never the less equally telling. Jesus set the standard for justice. He called us to confront evil and take action against evil. Psalms 82:3 says to give justice to the weak, the fatherless, the afflicted and destitute. Isaiah 1:17 told us to learn good and seek justice. Micah 6:8 asks the question what does the Lord require of you but to do justice. Luke 11:42 rebukes neglecting justice.

The traditional definition of social justice is one most would gladly agree is honorable. It is simply promoting a just society. The Biblical definition starts with reminded that all men are created in the image of God. (Erickson, 2018)The just end is the eternal end that all should seek. Living by Christ's commandments of redemption, sanctification and believing are the means. The use of the term social justice today is totally a temporal view in contrast to the Biblical view of eternity. The perfect justice will come one day. God heals us, redeems us and restores our being. The solution some suggest is continued prayer. Christianity today is fighting the battle and the best resource to use to maintain the Biblical understanding of justice is to pray and let God direct our actions. There are many things promoted under the banner of social justice today that are Biblical not so. The choices of people may be sinful and wrong and Christians frown upon such behavior. That does not mean Christians hate those who do such for Christians are commanded to love one another. The misrepresentation by progressive is that Christian disapproval is hate. It is not. It is disapproval. Disapproving and loving can exist in the same sphere.

Social Justice is misunderstood, applied erroneously and so often misused. Each of these has led to many judging Christianity as being a hate philosophy. Since this is indelibly incorrect how did everything get so skewed? Historically the term related to economic disparities within a society or culture. It became a subject of discussion in the early 1800's so it is not a newly created term. Only its definition is evolving. Originally the term was associated with a conservative approach to living. In the 1970's the term moved to be a liberal secular political philosophy. (Carter, 2018). Carter in his FAQ article just cited addresses how the fluid nature of the English language has allowed definitions of words and terms to part from their literal and primary meaning of denotation to obtaining an emotional meaning. This has been the route of the term social justice. Today it has abandoned its primary meaning that has historically been the norm to one that is used widely to stir emotions. One of the truest meanings comes from early Roman rule where justice itself is a situation where each gets his due. This definition states that one gets what they earn in a system that rewards one according to their contribution to cause. The liberal take on justice is defaulting to more accurately to the term "equal". Regardless of how much you contribute to a purpose or cause or piece of work, you get an equal amount of the whole. Those who contributed more get the same as those who contributed less. The Biblical view is that according to God's law one receives what is due them having contributed according to their unique ability. The early Hebrew meaning clearly establishes the principle of "equity" as the metric for justice. This is considerably different than the term "equal" It's been referred previously that there are two different takes on how these two terms imply a different approach to using the term justice for any purpose.

God knows the difference between equal and equitable. 2 Corinthians 5:10 says "For we must all appear before the judgment seat of Christ, so that each one may receive what is due for what he has done in the body, whether good or evil". We will be rewarded based upon what we have done which will vary from person to person. For some believing Christians that is good news. Our reward and/or punishment will not be equally distributed. In other words, our devotion will not be diluted by those who don't believe. For non-believers, they will be wishing their judgement might be lessen by an equal distribution instead of an equitable distribution. Ephesians 6:8 further emphasizes that what we receive back from the Lord will associated with whatever good we have done. Again, not an equal reward but an equitable one.

The New Testament Matthew 16:27 adds more credence to the notion of equitable distribution by articulating: "For the Son of Man is going to come with his angels in the glory of his Father, and then he will repay each person according to what he has done." As liberalism and progressives advocate an equal distribution of not only wealth but also non-financial rights, it is in direct contradiction to the Bible. The Scriptures demand we be generous to the less fortunate but without sacrificing to the point that we become impoverished ourselves. Social justice references in the Bible promote both public justice between individuals and justice involving associations such as governments.

During the 20th Century, denominations began to adopt a cultural social justice platform to the decline of gospel justice. As liberalization pervaded certain denominations, membership decline soon followed. Abandonment of Biblical justice has had its price. Current polls show that people desire authenticity from the pulpit. They want instruction from the pulpit. When going to church is no different than going to theater or high school ball game, people wonder why go to church. The churches must counter the naivety of today's social justice definition with a return to Biblical justice and it must be core to every message from a pulpit. Two extractions from Joe Carter's FAQs (Carter, 2018) article speak volumes. The first quote is credited to Don Carson (Carson, 2010). "The gospel is the good news of what God has done, especially in Christ Jesus, especially in his cross and resurrection; it is not what we do. Because it is news, it is to be proclaimed. But because it is powerful, it not only reconciles us to God, but transforms us, and that necessarily shapes our behavior, priorities, values, relationships with people, and much more. These are not optional extras for the extremely sanctified, but entailments of the gospel. To preach moral duty without the underlying power of the gospel is moralism that is both pathetic and powerless; to preach a watered-down gospel as that which tips us into the kingdom, to be followed by discipleship and deeds of mercy, is an anemic shadow of the robust gospel of the Bible; to preach the gospel and social justice as equivalent demands is to misunderstand how the Bible hangs together."

A second meaningful insight from Carter's FAQs beyond his C. S. Lewis quote is from Charles Colson's 1994 book The Body. "'Fundamentalism' is really akin to [C. S.] Lewis's 'mere Christianity' . . . it means adherence to the fundamental facts—in this case, the fundamental facts of Christianity," Charles Colson said. "Everyone who believes in the orthodox truths about Jesus Christ—in short, every Christian—is a fundamentalist. And we should not shrink from the term nor allow the secular world to distort its meaning." Do not let the secular world distort Christianity. This is the objective of the current social justice movement today.

Church Advocacy

The church's advocacy should be true social justice on issues like abortion, religious freedom, human suffering, peaceful coexistence among people of all color and aid to the disadvantaged. If all people are created in God's image, then our treatment of people is by creation our treatment of God. Matthew 7:12 gives us the rule that everyone should adhere: "So whatever you wish that others would do to you, do also to them, for this is the Law and the Prophets. "A simple fix to the political debate on social issues could easily be reconciled by following Matthew 7:12. How would you feel if what you are inflicting on someone else was inflicted on you. There is an abundance of name calling that transpires in the discussion of social justice and it divides people and causes entrenchment in their belief. Words carry power and in the present social climate, words can hurt. There's no better place to turn than to Proverbs on the issue of "words". The following are subtle reminders of the grace of speech and the power of speech:

Proverbs 18:21 "Death and life are in the power of the tongue, and those who love it will eat its fruits."

Proverbs 12:18 "There is one whose rash words are like sword thrusts, but the tongue of the wise brings healing."

Proverbs 15:1 "A soft answer turns away wrath, but a harsh word stirs up anger."

Proverbs 16:24 "Gracious words are like a honeycomb, sweetness to the soul and health to the body."

Proverbs 21:23 "Whoever keeps his mouth and his tongue keeps himself out of trouble."

Proverbs 13:3 "Whoever guards his mouth preserves his life; he who opens wide his lips comes to ruin."

Proverbs 15:4 "A gentle tongue is a tree of life, but perverseness in it breaks the spirit."

Proverbs 10:19 "When words are many, transgression is not lacking, but whoever restrains his Proverbs 18:20 "From the fruit of a man's mouth his stomach is satisfied; he is satisfied by the yield of his lips."

Proverbs 25:11 "A word fitly spoken is like apples of gold in a setting of silver."

Proverbs 11:12 "Whoever belittles his neighbor lacks sense, but a man of understanding remains silent."

Proverbs 18:13 "If one gives an answer before he hears, it is his folly and shame."

Proverbs 17:9 "Whoever covers an offense seeks love, but he who repeats a matter separates close friends."

Proverbs 29:20 "Do you see a man who is hasty in his words? There is more hope for a fool than for him."

Proverbs 15:2 "The tongue of the wise commends knowledge, but the mouths of fools pour out folly."

Proverbs is a wonderful book in the Bible for behavioral and moral guidance but Ephesians 4:29 also has some words of wisdom to consider: "Do not let any unwholesome talk come out of your mouths, but only what is helpful for building others up according to their needs, that it may benefit those who listen." This statement is the mantra of anyone in the field of education.

And let us not forget how powerful the ultimate Word is: Hebrews 4:12: "For the word of God is living and active, sharper than any two-edged sword, piercing to the division of soul and of spirit, of joints and of marrow, and discerning the thoughts and intentions of the heart."

Seeking Justice

Three things define our understanding of social justice. The first is that we are sinners. Each and every one of us should have God's justice served on us. The scriptures say that "none is righteous, no, not one". Yet we must continue to better understand the justice that Jesus taught and strive to emulate His characterization of justice. Asking God to serve justice is asking Him to use His glory to make right what is wrong. We observe activities in our world, and we think these things are wrong. Others think they are right. In the end, God will decide.

The second concept in understanding Biblical justice is to retreat to the one basic element of Christianity and that is Jesus died for our sins. He sacrificed to render true justice and it will come to everyone. The ultimate social justice was Jesus suffering the full justice of God's judgement for our sins. His death and resurrection created the path so that we may join in the righteousness of God. (Young, 2019)

Social justice is not a religion. It is not etched in stone. The principles of justice in the Gospel are clearly defined and society is not at liberty to change the Gospel's definition. They may try, and society may be gullible enough to let them but, in the end, one must hope that the churches stand firm against them by an unwavering commitment to the Word of God.

Human Rights not Social Justice

One element of social justice that gets overlooked by the promotion of the progressive vogue issues of the day is its commandment on human rights. Human rights are in search for a definition of its own. It seems that the inalienable rights our founding fathers insisted were irrevocable by any lesser power than God are in need of a modern-day definition. Progressives think that sin is an inalienable right. Homosexuality, cultural worship of fame and fortune, abortion and inequality within a population are all human rights that must be accepted by everyone. The social justice push has been to seek ways to enforce their view of rights onto everyone. The following from the Bible Project explains human rights is its simplest philosophical form: "In Genesis, we see that human beings were made "in the image of God".

This means to say that humans were created to be God's representatives on earth and carry out His plan, abiding by the morals and concepts of justice that God himself abides by. According to the Biblical justice that God sets forth, all humans are equal, all humans are created in His image, and all humans deserve to be treated with fairness and justice.

Of course, as we all know, human beings do not always behave this way. Instead, even in the earliest parts of the Bible, we see humans rejecting God's principles of Biblical justice and instead begin defining good and evil for themselves in a way that gives them advantages over others. The strong take advantage of the vulnerable, both at an individual level and at a societal level. Throughout all of this, the justice that God intended for people to exhibit is nowhere to be found.

Out of this mess, though, God raises up a man named Abraham and positions him to start a new line of people with his family-one that is ruled by both righteousness and justice. So, what does God mean when he tells Abraham and his people to live their lives with righteousness and justice? In the Bible, righteousness refers to a state of moral good in which you treat those around you with decency and fairness, recognizing that all of them are made in the image of God just like you.

While justice can be used to talk about retributive justice in which a person is punished for their wrongdoings, most of the time the Bible uses the word justice to refer to restorative justice, in which those who are unrightfully hurt or wronged are restored and given back what was taken from them. Taken this way, the combination of righteousness and justice that God dictates means a selfless way of life in which people do everything they can to ensure that others are treated well, and injustices are fixed." (What the Bible says about "Human Rights" and "Social Justice", 2019).

The social justice conflagration with human rights is the consensus of the objective. One group's view is a utilitarian world existence that strives to have Eden back again as it was before the Fall. The progressive and liberal groups only want to deal with individual rights in so much to say that anything goes. The conservative perspective emphasizes morality. (Holmes, 2018)With such divergent objectives, its little wonder that the divisiveness being experienced today is what it is. How can we return to an era of destigmatizing people and following the commandment of loving all? God's instruction on justice is just that. It is thinking critically, maintaining the Biblical view, loving your neighbor, assist communities, accepting that "rights" are equal and the guideline is morality. It is said that your rights end where mine begin. This buffer has provided the balance of human existence historically and should be instituted behavior that each individual follow.

Accepted Definition, Wrong Definition

An examination of how social justice, AKA human rights, has become a politically charged concept that no one can agree upon what it is they are addressing. Wikipedia, being an open source vehicle, has this modern-day definition that shows how confusing the discussion has become. From Wikipedia: "Social justice is also a concept that some use to describe the movement towards a socially just world. In this context, social justice is based on the concepts of human rights and equality and involves a greater degree of economic egalitarianism through progressive taxation, income redistribution, or even property redistribution. These policies aim to achieve what developmental economists refer to as more equality of opportunity than may currently exist in some societies, and to manufacture equality of outcome in cases where incidental inequalities appear in a procedurally just system."

Key words in this definition demonstrate how far the social justice movement of today is so distant than the Biblical concepts espoused in so many scriptures. First is term "egalitarianism". This is an economic philosophy associated with communism and socialism. In simple terms, it's take from those that have and give to those who don't in disregard to how those that have got what they have. Income redistribution and property redistribution are in the definition. "The Catechism of the Catholic Church defines the virtue of justice (n. 1807): "Justice is the moral virtue that consists in the constant and firm will to give their due to God and neighbor. Justice toward God is called the "virtue of religion." Justice toward men disposes one to respect the rights of each and to establish in human relationships the harmony that promotes equity with regard to persons and to the common good." (Pilote, 2014). Their adaptation of the word "equity" is paramount in understanding true social justice.

2 Corinthians 9:6-8 speaks of giving but it also defines how one accumulates their harvest: "Remember this: Whoever sows sparingly will also reap sparingly, and whoever sows generously will also reap generously. Each one should give what he has decided in his heart to give, not out of regret or compulsion. For God loves a cheerful giver. And God is able to make all grace abound to you, so that in all things, at all times, having all that you need, you will abound in every good work...." Romans 2:6 makes a similar statement though it is in the context of doing righteousness: "God "will repay each one according to his deeds." 1 Corinthians 3:8 is more to the point: "Now he who plants and he who waters are one; but each will receive his own reward according to his own labor." This means not only one's Heavenly reward but also ones' earthly reward.

The Defining Difference

A defining difference between Biblical social justice and the social justice society is promoting is the Bible puts the onus of justice on the individual and the contemporary form of social justice of today is advocating that government should render justice. The Bible repeatedly advocates helping the poor, the widow, the disadvantage and disabled. It makes clear that this is an individual Christian responsibility. Biblical social justice requests that one do what they can to whom they choose to help. Governmental social justice says that beaurocrats will decide who must give the help and to whom it will be given. History has shown that the denying of wealth creation leads to governmental downfalls. It has also shown us that forcing people to support actions and entities that they don't support eventually leads to major civil unrest. Galatians 3:28 states, "There is neither Jew nor Gentile, neither slave nor free, nor is there male and female, for you are all one in Christ Jesus". Christian justice is blind to differences in social status and God is concerned about distinctions. It was Jesus who inspired Christian social justice and not a liberal movement or mass media promulgation. Our approach to social justice should be as this writer advocates: "Instead of being motivated by political affiliations, financial gain, power, pride, control, or our own secular motivations, we should be active participants for the sake of following Jesus — for the purpose of glorifying God by through acts of justice, empowerment, and love." (Mattson, 2015).

A good summary of the phenomenon of government power and political elite power is from *Thinking Faith*: "According to the vision set out in the Bible, the totalitarian exercise of power always leads to social injustice. Only by broadening its horizons to include more than the particular interests of specific individuals or groups can a society establish socially just foundations. This has been demonstrated historically and in the modern era, not only by systems of neo-liberalism, but also by nationalist and communist totalitarian systems, which have been seen to collapse during recent decades. Biblical texts take a very critical view of the kings of Israel, who represent national power. This is seen clearly in the story of the people of Israel's wish to have a king ruling over them (1 Sam 8) as well as in the narrative of the fall of the kingdom (2 Kings 24-25). The true king of Israel and of the whole world is God himself (cf. Ps 95-99)." (Markl, 2011). Markl also provides some Scripture to accentuate the Bible's emphasis on social justice:

Exodus 3:1-10 – God calls Moses to lead Israel out of Egypt.

Exodus 20:1-17 – The Ten Commandments

Psalm 10 – Rise, O God! Do not forget the oppressed!

Psalm 147 – Praise of God for his creation and for rescuing the oppressed

Isaiah 35 – Those rescued by God return to Zion full of joy.

Amos 5:7-15 – Accusation of injustice and motivation to charity

Matthew 6:24-34 – God cares for you – care you for his kingdom!

Luke 10:25-37 – Main commandment and parable of the Good Samaritan

1 Corinthians 12:12-27 – You are one body with many members!

A contemporary look at the rise of a socialist platform in the United States shows how the current model of social justice is in conflict with the Biblical view of social justice. First, the current discussion with an impending Presidential election in 2020 is all about what the government can decide better than the individual. Secondly, the expansive list of potential candidates appears adamant that the solution is tax the wealthy into elimination and redistribute to those of governmental choice. A third departure is that government and not God can establish a utopia environment. Their most egregious objective is believing that they can control a population that is educated to the point of disagreement and equipped with the knowledge that God has always corrected His people when they stray from His commandments and directives. Perhaps they disbelieve history and in particularly Biblical history.

B. J. Campbell in his article "Social Justice is a Crowdsourced Religion" (Campbell, 2018)had the following to say about the crucial need for America to come to grasp with social justice in its current application. "Future historians chronicling the Grand American Culture War of the Twenty Teens will identify three mostly distinct factions. The Blue Tribe, who vies for control so they may push Blue values on others, the Red Tribe, who vies for control to push Red values on others, and the Grey Tribe, who hides in the corner with a bowl of popcorn trying to figure out what the heck is going on. And across the vast theater of this war, the hottest battleground, and the one most deserving of analysis, we might collectively call "Social Justice.""

He continues to highlight what may be the feature that has a stranglehold on the divisiveness we see today. That hold is in communication and hearing what might not be what is actually said. It's an interesting take on the communication problem. Of note is the word "equity" comes back into play. "There are many important additional parallels. Religions have a tendency to identify everything good with God, so when a religious person hears an atheist say they don't believe in God, the religious person has a tendency to *hear* that to mean they don't believe in *Good*. Social Justice followers react the same way. When someone questions their equity driven approach to "equality," that's *"hate speech.""* (Campbell, 2018). It is the inflexible ideology that both sides hold that make finding a middle ground and a peaceful coexistence that presents the barrier. Social justice advocates today have a religion and it is their commitment to a cause. The error of their ways seems to be in their presentation. There are so many areas and principles that all sides; the Blue, the Red and the Grey, can agree on that if they could find a common language to use then the chaos around the very discussion might attain a more civil discourse.

An undertaking by James A. Lindsay and Mike Nayna, "Postmodern Religion and the Faith of Social Justice," in Aero can be read here: https://areomagazine.com/2018/12/18/postmodern-religion-and-the-faith-of-social-justice/

It's over 15,000 words. Whether agree or disagree, their analysis adds insight. For brevity, they broke their discussion into these categories that give a suitable overview.

- **Social Justice and Religion** – What I intend to say and not say about whether Social Justice is best thought of as a religion—mostly housekeeping and a bit dry
- **Ideologically Motivated Moral Communities** – A Durkheimian view of the religion-like sociocultural phenomenon to which both Social Justice and religions belong

- **Religions Meet Needs** – An elaboration on the previous section that explains why human beings organize into ideologically motivated moral communities

- **Social Justice Institutionalized** – A presentation of how Social Justice exhibits institutionalization, which is central to organized religions

- **The Scholarly Canon** – How academic scholarship in "grievance studies" serves as a scriptural canon for Social Justice

- **Faith in Social Justice** – An exposition on faith and its role in the Social Justice ideology

- **The Mythological Core of Applied Postmodernism** – A lengthy discussion of mythology inside and outside of religion and how postmodernism and its currently ascendant derivatives fit into this framework. (If you really want to understand the deepest part of this essay, it's probably in this section, which can be read first if desired.)

- **Pocket Epistemologies** – A discussion of the means by which an ideological tribe aims to legitimize the "special knowledge" that serves it and how this manifests in Social Justice

- **A Focus on the Unconscious** – A more focused discussion upon the methods of special knowledge production of ideological tribes and the postmodern numinous experience

- **Ritual, Redemption, and Prayer** – A short section about the role these play in ideological tribes and how they manifest in Social Justice

- **Gender Nuns and the Grand Wizards of the Diversity Board** – Addresses the function of the priest caste within ideological tribes, including Social Justice, and how they put their faith into practice

- **Summary** – A short summary of the case made about whether Social Justice constitutes a religion. TL; DR: Yes and no, and mostly yes.

- **What Can We Do with This?** – A brief discussion of secularism, construed much more broadly than usual, and how it applies to dealing with a very religion-like Social Justice

THE CULTURAL CHURCH

Cultural Change

Concern is expressed about the church being in decline. The question is whether Christianity is in decline and that answer seems to be NO. The same cannot be said about church attendance. World Christianity is growing as stated in this statistic from Christian Headlines in January, 2019: "As 2019 begins, the world is becoming more religious, not less. Faith from diverse traditions grows as population expands throughout most of the Global South. Last year, nearly 50 million more Christians were added in Africa, making it the continent with the most adherents to Christianity in the world, 631 million." (Granberg-Michael, 2019). One will recall that it was the African attendees at the United Methodist Conference that swung the denomination's vote to hold to strict Biblical doctrines on homosexuality and some other social variants.

It's not necessarily other religious groups that are gaining ground as discovered in the results of a December, 2018 Public Religion Research Institute (PRRI) survey. "Non-Christian religious groups are growing, but they still represent less than one in ten Americans combined. Jews constitute 2% of all Americans while Muslims, Buddhists, and Hindus each constitute only 1% of the public. All other non-Christian religions constitute an additional 1%." (Daniel Cox, 2017).

The question is one of semantics. What question is being asked? Are we talking percentages or real numbers? It seems that there is still growth consistent with the world population growth as seen in this 2018 Pew survey: "In the last 100 years, the number of Christians in the world has quadrupled from about 600 million in 1910 to more than 2 billion presently. Today, Christianity is the world's largest religious group. According to the Pew Forum on Religion and Public Life, in 2010, there were 2.2 billion Christians of all ages living in the world." (Fairchild, 2018). The survey also generated this statistic: "Today in the U.S., about 78% of adults (247 million) identify themselves as Christian. In comparison, the next largest religions in America are Judaism and Islam. Combined they represent less than three percent of the United States population."

Two observations can be made by these types of polls. First is that there is generational ebb and flow regarding church attendance. Young people leaving home for the first time have always shied away from church attendance. This has not changed in decades. As this groups get older, marry and have a family, they tend to migrate back to church attendance. This movement is not easy to track in a poll. The second observation is that of technology. Brick and mortar churches just like brick and mortar colleges and universities are becoming less popular and electronic sources are replacing what once was only attainable inside a building. Television was the first to have an impact but today the internet has taken over a good portion of both church attendance and college and university attendance. Higher education has its fair share of only partially filled dormitories as well.

The younger generation, the Millennials and Generation Z, were born in the instant information age. They may well keep this preference when they again return to their family roots and church attendance at a building may be in a "forever" decline. Perhaps it is not just cultural changes that are influencing church statistics but also what is happening inside the church. These two paragraphs from a Barna research group in early 2014 point to an internal issue. "Perhaps more poignant than reasons not to turn up for church are the motivations of those who do, swimming upstream against the cultural current. Adults who believe church is very important cite two reasons above the rest: to be closer to God (44%) and to learn about God (27%). One in five (22%) say they go to church because the Bible teaches fellowship with other believers. And in spite of a growing epidemic of loneliness, just one in 10 report going to church because they are looking for community."

"Although people cite their primary reasons for attending church as growing closer to God and learning more about him, Barna Group finds such closeness is a rare occurrence. Fewer than two out of 10 churchgoers feel close to God on even a monthly basis. Additionally, while almost two-thirds of those who value church attendance go to learn more about God, fewer than one in 10 (6%) who have ever been to church say they learned something about God or Jesus the last time they attended. In fact, the majority of people (61%) say they did not gain any significant or new insights regarding faith when they last attended."

"The data shows two trends, often at crosscurrents. Adults are aware of their very real spiritual needs, yet they are increasingly dissatisfied with the church's attempt to meet those spiritual needs and are turning elsewhere." (Americans Divided on the Importance of Church, 2014).

Should the discussion to reverse a declining interest in Christianity start with a return to authentic Biblical teachings? Polls have indicated that people thrive on authenticity. They sense it and know what it is. The Bible is authentic. We must remember the very basics of the Bible and always work from the premise of known facts. The foundational principles that must return to the church are these inerrant facts from Michael Morrison, Dean of Faculty and Professor of New Testament at Grace Communion Seminary: "Affirmation: God has all authority, and we accept the Bible as the primary authority by which God communicates to us what God wants us to believe and to do. The New Testament clarifies and sometimes supersedes the Old Testament guidance on faith and life. The primary purpose of the Bible is its message about salvation, and that is its primary sphere of authority. It is a sufficient guide that tells us how we are given eternal life with God and how we should respond. Those who believe the biblical revelation about God's grace and Jesus Christ enjoy the salvation he has given; unbelievers do not (John 3:18; 14:6; Acts 4:12; 1 John 5:11-12). This message of salvation is essential."

"The Scriptures are a trustworthy guide for our relationships with God and with other humans. They give truth about faith, worship, salvation, morals and ethics (2 Timothy 3:15-16). But biblical commands cannot be applied simplistically, because some are superseded, and some apply only in limited situations. We seek the illumination of the Holy Spirit and ask God to guide our reasoning and our use of tradition and experience, so we might understand how to apply biblical principles."

"The Bible is an authoritative revelation of truths about God, and we want to worship our Creator with as much understanding as possible. Moreover, we want to obey God's commands, not only to honor God but also because we believe that our all-wise and perfectly loving Creator has given us the best possible commands and guidance for life. Therefore, we want to understand the written message of God as best we can." (Morrison, 2019).

Morrison mentions the truths that must come from the pulpit. Every Systematic Theology text emphasizes these four characteristics of scripture: Authority, Clarity, Necessity and Sufficiency. (Gruden, 1994).

Stand Tall

Today's pulpits are seemingly short on authenticity when it comes to the hard facts of the Bible that go against the modern cultural trend. Antisemitism is being demonstrated in the halls of Congress and gets little push back. It is a hate crime in certain countries to express your opinion about homosexuality, Islam, abortion but not Christianity. These are warning signs that a part of the global culture is moving rapidly against the teachings of the Bible. The pulpit has to counter this swing in direction. Authenticity is the key. People know authenticity when they see it and hear it. Authenticity should not be mistaken for relativism which is what the progressive cultural population wishes people to think. Ephesians 4:22-24 addresses the transformation of the false illusion of your old life and your authentic life achievable by the grace of God. It reads in part: "…to put off your old self, which belongs to your former manner of life and is corrupt through deceitful desires, and to be renewed in the spirit of your minds, and to put on the new self, created after the likeness of God in true righteousness and holiness."

Polls point to a population of believers that are wanting the facts. Not the watered down, politically correct message from the pulpit so that everyone has that feel good feeling about being so nice and accepting. Acts 2:42 recalls a similar group of people. They were eager to hear the message and the leaders taught the message authentically. Mike Livingstone emphasized this fundamental in his blog: "Let's be clear about what we mean by "Bible teaching." Teaching the Bible goes beyond using a biblical passage as a peg on which to hang good ideas. Bible teaching approaches the Bible in such a way that allows the biblical text to set the agenda and to speak for itself. What God has said in His Word is what we must teach." (Livingstone, 2016).

Livingstone continued with these five reasons the church must teach the Bible and not surrender to the politically correct pressures of progressivism. First is because the Bible is God's Word. Secondly, it is God's authoritative Word. Third, the Bible is sufficient. It contains all that God meant for us to have in the guidance of our lives. The fourth reason is that teaching the Bible is required. We are not only to read the Bible, but it also requires that we all help spread the Word, to be evangelists and missionaries in our own right. The fifth reason is the church must truly feel that their services are needed. As Livingstone says, the church itself is filled with Biblical illiterates that are craving to learn the truth. Churches must not marginalize Biblical teachings. (Livingstone, 2016). 2 Timothy 3:16 further lists the usages of Scripture: "All Scripture is breathed out by God and profitable for teaching, for reproof, for correction, and for training in righteousness,".

Christians must establish their authenticity as individuals before advancing to convince others of the authentic nature of the Bible. A Bible.org series presented these principles as necessities for authentication: "Authentic Christians are marked by thankfulness and prayer, faith in Christ, love for the saints, and the hope of heaven."

"Someone has said, "Sincerity is the key to success. If you can fake that, you've got it made!" We're all prone to fake it, aren't we! It's not spiritually healthy to be overly introspective, but sometimes it is good to do an inside checkup. Paul exhorts (2 Cor. 13:5), "Test yourselves to see if you are in the faith; examine yourselves! Or do you not recognize this about yourselves, that Jesus Christ is in you—unless indeed you fail the test?" So, ask yourself, "Is my Christianity authentic or am I faking it?" Here are the tests:

Am I marked by *thankfulness* and *prayer*? Is my *faith in Jesus Christ* and *His gospel*? Am I working at genuine *love* for all of God's people, especially those I rub shoulders with every day? Am I motivated in all I do by the *hope* laid up for me in heaven?" (Cole S. J., 2015). Perfection in these things is not required or possible in this life. But to be authentic Christians, we should be working at and making progress in thankfulness and prayer; faith in Christ and the gospel; love for one another; and the hope laid up for us in heaven." (Livingstone, 2016).

Authenticity is the key to retention and perhaps even recruitment. In academia, retention is first on the priority list and second is recruitment. It takes both to have and maintain a vibrant student body. Reviewing again the quantitative news coming from polls, the facts seem to be pointing in one direction. These reports as recent as 2016:

"Overall, the Church's influence on Americans is beginning to fade. A growing number of Americans have given up on God—or at least on organized religion. They have become "Nones," a term popularized by Pew Research. And their numbers are growing.

Pew's 2007 Religious Landscape study, which surveyed 35,000 respondents, found that about 16% of Americans claimed no religious affiliation. By 2015, that number had grown to 23%, almost one in four Americans.

Gallup, another well-respected national firm, gives a wider view of the rise of the Nones. In 1967, Gallup found that about 2% of Americans—or 1 out of every 50—claimed no religious preference. By 2014, that number had grown to 16%, or about 1 in 7.

Pew has also tracked the decline in the percentage of Americans who claim to be Christians. In 2007, Pew found that about 8 in 10 Americans identified as Christians. That number dropped to 7 in 10 in 2014—a statistically significant change in a relatively short time. Pew also found that less than half of Americans (46.5%) now identify as Protestants for the first time in American history." (Stetzer, 2016).

These numbers represent half-truths if read independently of the sidebar statistics that accompany other polls questioning a similar phenomenon. The General Social Survey (GSS) began in 1972 and has tracked religious tradition. A different picture emerges from the GSS surveys. Using the religious tradition rational and dating to the 1940's, church attendance stood at 37% of Americans at that time. In 2015, the same rational found that 36% of Americans attended church. Not a dramatic decline in over 70 years. Using the same GSS findings, Protestant church attendance has declined from 23% to 20% over the past 40 years. Again, not an avalanche of decline. (Stetzer, 2016). It seems Americans remain devout Christians though the popular media relentlessly tries to paint an opposite picture.

But take warning in the trend. This beckons the question again about how churches can retain membership and attendance and recruit more members. Here the polls must be taken with some credence. It's being authentic, avoid the temptation of sweetening the Scriptures to be alluring to a politically correct culture, teach the Word as God gave it to us with no editing, demonstrate authentic Christianity as an individual, praying, having faith and believing in Jesus Christ and His Word.

2018 Breakpoint Symposium

The 2018 Breakpoint symposium dealt with the many issues confronted today's church and Christianity. It is worthy to note some of the comments made by the many panelist discussing the church in 2018. This symposium was held in January 2018 and it is interesting to have witnessed many of the events and activities mentioned by the panelist as 2018 ended and 2019 began. Ryan T. Anderson, William E. Simon Senior Research Fellow at

The Heritage Foundation, had this observation about the gender dysphoria that was headline news for much of 2018. "Properly understanding sex, gender, gender identity, and gender dysphoria will continue to be pressing concerns in 2018. A proper understanding is a prerequisite for properly forming people in the truth and properly ministering to people in need. As new gender ideologies are promoted throughout America, their lies will impact not only those who suffer from gender dysphoria, but all children who need to mature in their self-understanding as a boy or girl, man or woman, a potential husband or wife, father or mother."

Bruce Riley Ashford, Provost and Professor of Theology & Culture at Southeastern Baptist Theological Seminary, brought attention to Christianity being displaced by secularism with this comment: "One of the most pressing challenges for Western Christians is to explore the implications of our civilization's transition to a secular age. As Charles Taylor has argued, Christian belief has not only been displaced from the default position, but is aggressively contested by numerous other options. Christianity is merely one option among many, and an implausible and unimaginable one at that. Thus, Christians have a unique opportunity to reimagine our social, cultural, and political witness so that it speaks with salience to our secular age."

"There should be little question that Christians should not be immigration hawks of the "keep them out" variety simply because we believe in the brotherhood and sisterhood of men and women under the fatherhood of God. I don't say that to suggest nations should not have borders or some orderly process of immigration, but there is something wrong with a tribal sense of us v. them as we consider immigration across our long border with Mexico. Christians should be emphatically for the development of a reasonable and charitable resolution of the problem and for the victims (such as the "dreamers") to find access to a good way forward. Have the laws been broken? Absolutely, but in the case of dreamers they had no choice in what their parents did. That matters in the moral analysis." This was Hunter Baker, J.D., Ph.D., associate professor of political science at Union University and a fellow of the Ethics and Religious Liberty

Commission, take on the immense immigration issue that is never ceasing to this day.

A very telling observation was made by Bill Brown, PhD, Senior Fellow for Worldview and Culture, The Colson Center. "The descent into a self-identity obsessed culture has diminished us. *Who* you are has no meaning; *what* you are, or say you are, is vital? The truth that each person is created in God's image is rejected in education, law, politics, popular culture, and even religion. The consequences are devastating."

Os Guinness, author "A Free People's Suicide" and the forthcoming "Last Call for Liberty" can the closest to predicting the difficult state of affairs Christianity would be in at the close of 2018 and into 2019. "If we fight the battle at any point except where the battle is really being fought, we might as well not fight. Luther's famous maxim is urgent for Christians today. The U.S. is experiencing its gravest crisis since the Civil War, but there is no agreement as to what the crux of the battle is. The division in this country is not just between Progressives and Conservatives, "coastals" and "heart-landers," and "globalists" and "nationalists." It is between "1776," and the heirs and allies of the American revolution, where faith and freedom went hand in hand; and "1789," and the heirs and allies of the thinking of the French revolution, where faith and freedom were mortal enemies.

The current crisis is a tale of these two revolutions. Both cry "freedom," but their views of freedom are diametrically opposed. They have different roots (the Bible versus the Enlightenment), different views of human nature (realism versus utopianism), different views of change (incremental versus radical), different views of freedom (the power to do what you ought versus the permission to what you like), different views of government (protective versus Progressive), different views of accountability ("under God" versus without God), and different views of righting wrongs (repentance and reconciliation versus reparation and revenge). Guinness summed up the preceding observations by arriving at the end game for 2018.

These extractions from the Breakpoint symposium (Stonestreet, 2018) are representative of the actual issues confronted by Christians and the church during 2018 and remain unabated into 2019. Gender and sexual choice issues, secularism, immigration and the influx of non-Christian faiths as well as illegal immigration, self-identity culturalism and Os Guinness's thoughtful summary of the polarity of American population are as active in debate as they were a year ago. The church, (the ministry and the congregation), feel the need to be a counterbalance to these assaults but are lacking a cohesive platform and medium by which to be as vocal for Christianity as the opposing secular forces are. There is hardly any mention of Christianity in the main street media except that which is negative. Christian advocates are rarely given a forum to present their views while the news is saturated with items that are counter Christian.

Church Countermeasures

The church, the whole body of Christ's church, is not without resources and means to counter secularism and progressivism. As with any effort to counter a movement it is imperative to have a good understanding of the philosophy and motives driving the movement. Secularism is not necessarily an abandonment of spirituality. Religious practices are changing as the electronic realm of communications is changing. Many people still say they are spiritual, just not religious. Spiritualism is personal choice and faith will be less of a public institution or force in daily decisions. Personal choice as compared to doctrine adherence means people choose what feels right at the time. Religion is becoming privatized and faith is more experiential.

For secularist, religion as practiced in the past is not making sense anymore. Millennials see contradiction in doctrinal religion. How can one love your neighbor but say they are living in sin? Secularism removes God from any equation. Secularist cannot see a just God and a loving God as being a coherent situation. They have difficulty in the belief that God is very much a part of human existence. Science and media have strived to impress that man is in control of everything and that there is no guiding Master to today's living. They disregard the Old Testament stories and warnings as something resurrected from mythical imaginations. The cultural forces of today impress upon society that they should be free to do anything they choose. To have the lifestyle they desire, to act as they wish, to disregard rules and to condemn anyone who has opposing views to theirs is what secularism wishes to make normal. Utopia does not exist outside of God.

Churches must understand these driving forces and counteract these ideas and beliefs with a more forceful voice of the truth. Thomas Massaro, Core Christianity, elaborated on the aforementioned issue and closed with this message: "Our worship, liturgies, churches, and families must graciously point to the goodness of God, his beauty, and truth for which we were made. Worship should point with wonder to what God has done in the world, so we can see his good providence and grace in our daily lives." (Massaro, 2017).

Christians and the church must be engaged in what is happening. Bill Muehlenberg addressed these pressing facts in his Culture Watch letter in February 2019. "We live in not just a post-Christian culture but an anti-Christian one. All over the West it seems that Christianity – at least the biblical version – is under attack and often in retreat. The attacks on the faith have been relentless over the past century or so."

"We are seeing more and more restrictions on religious freedom and expression, and much of this is done under the guise of "hate crimes," "hate speech" and the like. Often to simply stand up for one's religious convictions will be deemed to be hateful, bigoted and intolerant."

"Bullying, intimidation and ugly anti-Christian bigotry is sadly now becoming the norm. If certain people are offended when a Christian or a Jew for example publicly defends their faith tradition on things like marriage and family, they have to learn to live with it. Seeking to shut down and censoring such speech and beliefs puts us on the road to the end of democracy and freedom." (Muehlenberg, 2019).

Rick Wade in Probe for Answers made the following comment in 2007 on perspective and viewing our existence in a secular environment that was even then making inroads into our culture: "Rather than seeing the secular world, the world we can see and touch, through a sacred lens, we're more apt to look at the sacred through a secular lens. May God help us to see all of life—including our clothes, our humor, our entertainment, our vocation, our relationships, and all the rest—through the eyes of God, as belonging to Him, and give us the resolve to bring them under His lordship." (Wade, 2007).

As far back as 1995, M. M. Thomas made the following remarks to theology students at the Federation of theological seminaries in Kerala at the Orthodox Theological Seminary, Kottayam on 14 Dec.95. "I believe that the Christian contribution to a "secular" concept of humanity as essentially a Community of Persons can be best made if we maintain the message of the gospel that God became incarnate in the Person of Jesus Christ to overcome the alienation of humanity from God and to create a *Koinonia in Christ* around the Eucharist, a Community of divine forgiveness and mutual forgiveness acknowledging Jesus Christ as Lord and Saviour, transcending all religious cultural and ideological divisions with a mission to build a wider *Secular Koinonia* of mutual forgiveness and justice among the peoples of the world, as witness to the ultimate goal of creation, namely the Kingdom of God." (Thomas, 1995). Koinonia is Christian fellowship or communion, with God or, more commonly, with fellow Christians.

A good summation of secularism's evolvement comes from a 2008 interview in the Enrichment journal. These statements on secularism's evolution are by Ravi Zacharias. "First, secularization generally held that religious ideas, institutions, and interpretations have lost their social significance. People liked the idea of a secular society and a secular government. But in terms of moral values and ethics, they never checked into the internal assumptions of secularization that made it wide open to almost any view on any subject. Beginning in the 1960s, the moods of secularization ultimately led to society's loss of shame.

Next is pluralization, which sounds like a practical and worthy idea; and in many ways, it is. In pluralism you have a competing number of worldviews that are available, and no worldview is dominant. But smuggled in with pluralization was the absolutization of relativism. The only thing we could be sure of was that all moral choices were relative and there was no point of reference to right and wrong. This resulted in the death of reason.

Last is privatization, which is an accommodation to the religiously minded. If secularization and pluralization were going to hold sway, what does society do with the large number of people who are spiritually minded?

Being spiritually minded was okay as long as people kept their spiritual beliefs private and did not bring them into the public arena. The irony of this was the fact secularization — which had its assumptions on absolutes and anything of the metaphysical nature — was allowed into the public place. In fact, its very trust was to bring it into the public place. But anyone who believed in a spiritual Essence, an Ultimate Reality, and the fact there were transcendent absolutes that needed to be adhered to was told to keep those beliefs private. That ultimately paved the way for the loss of meaning." (Schoonover, 2008).

Review the Bible's Authenticity

In short form, these reminders from a Focus on Family article summarizes the authenticity of the Bible and how it is to be the foundational doctrines by which the church, in one way, combat secularism. "The entire Bible was written by about 40 individuals over 1,500 years. These writers included a farmer (Amos), a doctor (Luke), ministers (such as Ezra and James), political leaders (David, Solomon), political prisoners (Daniel, John), a musician (Asaph), a fisherman (Peter) and a tax collector (Matthew).

Moses, who wrote the first five books of the Old Testament, grew up wealthy in Egypt, became a fugitive, herded livestock, then eventually led a nation. Paul, who wrote 13 books of the New Testament, was professionally trained in religion, theology and philosophy, and before he became a Christian led a movement to hunt down the followers of Jesus Christ. The Bible writers were rich and educated, poor and not-so-educated; they came from a wide variety of social backgrounds.

Yet the Bible contains a unified, consistent message. It could be summarized as "God's Savior, and how you may know Him" or "The kingdom of heaven, and how to get in."

The agreement woven throughout all 66 books written by different people at different times strongly points to the Bible's heavenly origin. Though humans did the writing, the Bible is the product of one author: God.

Churches and Christians didn't choose the books they wanted to put in the Bible. They eventually recognized the books that God had chosen. Bible expert J. I. Packer puts it this way:

The church no more "gave us" the canon than Sir Isaac Newton "gave us" the force of gravity. God gave us gravity by the work of His creation, and similarly, He gave us the New Testament canon by inspiring the original books that make it up." (MacFarland, 2019).

Writer and TV personality Phil Robertson made this declaration in an interview with Breitbart News about the real direction America must pursue. "Trump wants to make American great again and I'm all for it and I'm behind him," Robertson assured listeners. He then laid out his own message: "I'm trying to get people to see that America is never going to be great again until they become at least godly again, that's my point." (Moons, 2019).

The recent news of high-profile celebrities and other elites bribing their children's way into elite universities provides another arrow in one's quiver when it comes to Biblical authenticity and dependability. The college admission scandal of 2019 is a reminder that those that stray from doctrine will a price to pay at some time and in some way. These scriptures speak of one of the main tenets of what Christianity is about. "But Scripture warns us: "Be sure your sin will find you out" (Numbers 32:23). God's word adds, "Whoever walks in integrity walks securely, but he who makes his ways crooked will be found out" (Proverbs 10:9). (Denison, 2019).

To present an authentic case for the Bible and its contents, we must emulate the Apostle Paul. These three reminders along with scripture if the church and believers are to wage an effective countermeasure to secularism and Christianity harassment. The first is our lives must be Gospel-centered, not me-centered. Secondly, our lives should model humility, not pride. Our Lives Must be Sincere. "Let these passages of Scripture resonate in your heart." (Baldwin, 2017).

2 Corinthians 6:4-6: "Instead, as God's ministers, we commend ourselves in everything: by great endurance, by afflictions, by hardships, by difficulties, by beatings, by imprisonments, by riots, by labors, by sleepless nights, by times of hunger, by purity, by knowledge, by patience, by kindness, by the Holy Spirit, by sincere love."

2 Corinthians 11:3: "But I fear that, as the serpent deceived Eve by his cunning, your minds may be seduced from a sincere and pure devotion to Christ."

1 Timothy 1:5: "Now the goal of our instruction is love that comes from a pure heart, a good conscience, and a sincere faith."

2 Timothy 1:5: "I recall your sincere faith that first lived in your grandmother Lois and in your mother Eunice and now, I am convinced, is in you also."

As mentioned in the MacFarland article, the authenticity of the Bible is indisputable. Some additional support lies in these facts. "Documentation. Thousands of ancient, hand-copied documents—referred to as "manuscripts"— provide proof of the New Testament and Old Testament's historical consistency. In fact, there is significantly more documentation for the books of the Bible than there are for other historically recognized authors and literature, such as Plato and *The Iliad*.

Archeological findings. Excavation sites and artifacts also provide evidence that many of the events, people and places mentioned in the Bible really existed—such as the city Jericho and its famous walls or the Hittites, a people group once thought by skeptics to be a myth.

The life of Jesus. The fact that Jesus was a true, historical person is clearly documented by Jewish manuscripts, even before Apostle Paul and the writers of Gospels provided their eye witness accounts. Other ancient cultural documents also reference his existence. For instance, the Roman leader and historian Tacitus wrote:

"Nero fastened the guilt and inflicted the most exquisite tortures on a class hated for their abominations, called Christians by the populace. Christus, from whom the name had its origin, suffered the extreme penalty during the reign of Tiberius at the hands of one of our procurators, Pontius Pilatus …"

Fulfilled prophecies. The Bible contains hundreds, even thousands, of prophecies that have been fulfilled, including detailed descriptions of events that would later happen to the Jewish people and surrounding nations, as well as prophecies about the life and death of Christ.

Redeemed lives. The Bible speaks to the condition of the human soul in a way that has life-changing impact on individuals from all cultures, nations and walks of life." (5 Evidences the Bible is True, 2019).

If more information is needed to validate the Bible, CBN News in April 2018 had an article by Paul Strand that solicited comments from Dr. Jonathan Morrow, Dr. Darrell Bock and Josh McDowell. The article was titled "Incredible Proof for Why You Should Have Faith in the Bible". (Strand, 2018). They list a myriad of reasons how it is that the Bible is one of the most authentic pieces of literature in the world. With all of the reasons to take the Bible as the Word of God and to understand its principles as the unadulterated truth for how we should live our lives, the church and its followers should have no reason to cower in the face of secularism. The church has to use all of the evidence of authenticity and push aggressively against the movements to minimize Christianity and its followers. Passivity will not work when the opposition is relentless. Instead of being on the defensive, churches must put Christianity on the offense.

VALUE JUDGING AND THE WORD

Matthew 25 has been a hot issue in the media and political world recently. Though mis referenced at times and misused more often, it warrants a review. Judging seems to be plentiful in the media among those that have a public stage. Setting off the scramble to the title of being more Christian was none other than Lady Gaga. In early January 2019 she made this announcement midway through one of her songs. This seemed to be the opening round of bringing the Bible into the political discussion of 2019. Expect it to get worse in 2020 as candidates vie for the Evangelical voter. Further captions reveal that Christianity is certainly being attacked on many fronts even to the point of making Christian comments illegal. Though not knocking on the door of the United States yet, the push to squelch Christian viewpoints using the law is gaining momentum. This chapter brings up incidences of value judging and how Christianity is being used inappropriately and inaccurately. First comes placing a value on one's degree of Christianity and then judging another's.

"Lady Gaga criticized Vice President Mike Pence Saturday for his support of a Christian school, saying he's the "worst representation" of the faith."

"To Mike Pence, who thinks it's acceptable that his wife work at a school that bans LGBTQ, you are wrong," she said, according to a YouTube video that was reported by Variety. "You say we should not discriminate against Christianity; you are the worst representation of what it means to be a Christian. I am a Christian woman and what I do know about Christianity is that we bear no prejudice, and everybody is welcome. So, you can take all that disgrace Mr. Pence and you can look yourself in the mirror and you'll find it right there." (Foust, 2019).

This was followed a couple of months later by both an inaccurate reference and a not so accurate interpretation of the Scripture that brings Matthew 25 into the discussion. Scripture is being used incorrectly to add validity to one's views. It is also being used by those being opportunistic without being honest. 2 Peter 1: 20-21 recounts the error of one's own interpretation: "Knowing this first of all, that no prophecy of Scripture comes from someone's own interpretation. For no prophecy was ever produced by the will of man, but men spoke from God as they were carried along by the Holy Spirit."

Democrat candidate for the Presidential primary made the following statement at one of her canvasing stops. "Elizabeth Warren says words of Jesus, judgement of 'sheep and goats,' is driving force in her life. "The story for me is Matthew 26 and I'm sure some of you, a lot of you know this story," she said incorrectly referencing the lesson of the judgement that comes in Matthew 25."

"You know this is the one where the Shepherd is dividing the world into the sheep and the goats. And as we all know, sheep are going to heaven, goats they're not. And the sheep asked Him, why us? Why us Lord? We look like those guys. And the Shepherd, the Lord answers back and says, 'I was hungry, and you gave me food. I was thirsty, and you gave me water, I was in prison and you visited me. Naked and you clothed me. And as much as you have done it to one of these, the least of thy brethren, you have done it unto me.' And what I hear in that is two things that guide me every day," Warren said." (Blair, 2019).

This of course is Mrs. Warren's justification for open borders and unlimited immigration. The misuse of Matthew 25 to support such advocacy will be rebutted later. The reference to Matthew 25 did not stop at the political podium but also made its way along with other Biblical references to the media. "MSNBC host Joe Scarborough says Trump is 'antithesis' of Bible's teachings in wake of Evangelical survey. Scarborough, whose cup has previous runneth over with critiques of the president, took things to a biblical level during a discussion regarding Evangelical support of Trump during "Morning Joe" on Tuesday."

"Evangelical Christians remain loyal to this man, and again, there is nothing consistent with the teachings of Jesus — and when I say nothing, I mean absolutely nothing. The Beatitudes, and the Sermon on the Mount, especially the story of the Good Samaritan." (Quinn, 2019).

If it is not bad enough to have the media and celebrities telling Christians how unchristian they are for not accepting their liberal interpretation of self, in Great Britain they even have the law on their side. This article was captured by the Christian Post: "Parents of autistic child threatened with removal of custody after rejecting puberty blockers. The parents of an autistic teen in England say they were threatened that their son would be removed from their custody following their objections about giving him puberty blockers. According to the Daily Mail Saturday, the parents of the teen, who spoke to the outlet on condition of anonymity, feared the potential side-effects of the drugs, and stopped him from going to a gender clinic as they suspected his sudden decision to pursue gender transition was due to his autism." (Showalter, 2019).

Again, in England, a Catholic journalist is being interrogated by police for 'misgendering' activist's transgender child. This was an innocent enough event given the whole story but there's no forgiveness when you cross the progressive line. Here's part of the story: "A Catholic journalist in England is being told by police that she might have committed a criminal offense because she "misgendered" someone and will soon be interrogated under caution. As far as the transgender ideology stretches, I believe it is one of complete submission. Those that even raise questions are silenced with threats and accusations of bigotry," Parker (the transgender activist laying the charge against Caroline Farrow) told CP in an interview last year weeks after her initial police interrogation. We all have the capacity to be offended and offensive. We have to decide whether we want to criminalize this offense," she added, noting that "in a world of billions I would hope the liberty of free speech is one we would extend to all, not just those we agree with." (Showalter, Christian journalist to be interrogated by police for 'misgendering' activist's transgender child, 2019).

The American public-school system is not above working against Christian doctrine and in several cases, openly inviting liberal and progressive dialog into the classroom. What makes this story even more ominous is that transgenderism is being introduced to kindergartners. "As the Daily Wire reported this week, an elementary school in Virginia conducted a brainwashing session with a group of kindergartners. The susceptible children were required to sit on the floor and listen to a cross-dressing man read a book promoting "transgenderism." The school claims it notified parents ahead of time about this event. The parents say otherwise. The lack of notification just makes the whole thing all the more outrageous, but it would still be outrageous even if the parents had all signed on."

"The brain is an organ of the body, it is part of the body. Saying a boy has a girl brain is like saying a boy has a girl pancreas or a girl elbow. If a boy's body is a boy body then his brain is automatically a boy brain, because his brain is not a separate organism from the body. The "transgender" advocates are proposing a very strange kind of dualism, whereby the human body can be bifurcated into girl parts and boy parts, and the various parts can be combined into one confused whole. This is superstition, not science. It is an item of faith, and a very weird faith at that." (Walsh, 2019).

A word about judging might reestablish the Christian's right to speak out against what they see as devaluing human actions. "Judge not, that you be not judged." – Matthew 7:1. This piece of Scripture is thrown in the face of Christians when Christians show disfavor and disdain at certain behavior. It is grossly misused outside of context further in the Bible. It is not warning us to withhold judging but just the opposite. When read in context with other Scripture, it describes a methodology for judging sin and calling sin for what it is. The caution in Matthew 7:1 is that such judging be done without being self-righteousness or hypocritical yourself.

Clarification of Matthew 25

To set the stage about the discussion of the contextual message of Matthew 25, verses 1 and 2 of Matthew 7 need to be recalled. They say in essence that good and truth ought not to be thought ill of and that man receives truth and good from the Lord, in proportion as he exercises them towards others. This message is used interchangeably with the word "charity" in Matthew 25. Matthew 25 is the judging of the nations. It is unsure if Senator Warren was using this piece of Scripture in relation to the United States being a nation or as a manner of personal behavior.

Some theorize that the separation of the nations into sheep and goats relates to how nations have treated their own population and not how they treat those wishing to come into their nation; i.e. immigrants. Following along this line, the nation gathering seems distinct from the great white throne referred to in Revelations 20:11-15. The great white throne judgment happens after the 1,000-year reign of Jesus Christ and His saints. The judgment of the nation's occurs immediately upon His return and is the subject of Matthew 25. The great white throne judgment happens in Heaven and the judgment of nations happens on earth. The judgment of nations may actually apply to how nations treat the Jewish people. Anti-Semitism is a boiling topic within American politics presently and the United States has always paid heed to the Christian philosophy of the nation of Israel being Biblically special. In today's Congress, they are factions that are blatantly anti-Israel. Believing in some of the interpretations of Matthew 25, anti-Israel is not in America's best interest since the judging of nations may be the process of Jesus setting aside those who support the Jewish nation and those who don't. The "my brethren" reference in Matthew 25 verse 40 may clearly mean Jesus's brethren, the Jews.

There are two divisions in Matthew, sheep and goats. This is the division of humanity. Debate remains as to how the population of earth will appear after the Great Tribulation. The rapture of the church will see many believers exiting earth. Persecution and martyrdom of believers after the rapture and during the Great Tribulation will see others departing earth. There will death and destruction during the Great Tribulation and Armageddon itself will diminish earth's population. For those that are left, Matthew 25 comes into play. For that population that remain on earth, the judgment of nations applies. At this time, the sheep will inherit the kingdom prepared for them. This group, the sheep, will be judged on the basis of their works. No mention of faith and forgiveness but judged on their moral kindness. There are names in the Book of Life as referenced in Revelations 20 and those names are a separate account. It is assumed that Matthew 25 is referencing judgment based upon mankind's humane treatment of others, particular the Christians and Jews who will suffer persecution and hatred during the Great Tribulation. Others such as the poor, the suffering and the under privileged may also enjoy Jesus's grace. Those not in good stead will be cast aside into everlasting punishment and the righteous into life eternal. (Guzik, 2018).

Other views are also applicable. The part of being hungry could be hungry for the Word of God. We are to share the Word. Being thirsty could be the water of the gospel as mentioned in John 4:14 and the stranger is clothed in righteousness and the prisoner is set free from Satan. This take on the Scripture takes its meaning out of the physical world interpretation and into the Heavenly world vision. The instruction to teach and spread the Word are mentioned in Acts 10:42 and Timothy 4:1. These are our works by which those remaining after Armageddon will be judged.

The second, third and fourth chapters of John present the tests for being Christian. Believe Jesus is the Son of God, follow His commandments and love fellow Christians. It is the later that belies the message of Matthew 25 judging of nations. Several writers interpret the judging of our work as being the following of His commandments, spreading His message and having a compassionate soul towards fellow Christians be they poor, imprisoned, needy, hungry or otherwise. The six works of mercy: Food, drink, hospitality, clothing, nursing care, and visitation are frequently mentioned in the Old Testament. These personal attributes are a product of a person's righteousness. Being righteous in the heart and having been transformed to such by believing in the Lord Jesus Christ brings forth the desire and will to practice the works of mercy.

A critique of the judging of nations concludes with this statement: "We are left with some ambiguity with regard to what Christ will do in a particular situation but no ambiguity with regard to our duty. We have a responsibility to tell people that Christ will bless those who show mercy to "the least of these *adelphon mou*— my brothers"—and to encourage them to watch for opportunities to minister (1) to needy people in general—(2) to needy Christians—and (3) to needy Christians engaged in the proclamation of the Gospel." (Donovan, 2009).

Scripture is frequently used to justify a liberal open border type of immigration policy. Matthew 25 and a multitude of others speaking of compassion towards the needy, widows and even foreigners or sojourners is put forth as the Christian necessity to welcome immigrants. Of lesser mention is the myriad of Scriptures that discuss nations and borders. The following by Frank Turek of Charisma News summarizes some of the mentioning of Biblical borders: "Finally, contrary to the media narrative, Scripture doesn't mandate open borders or prohibit walls. As Dr. Wayne Grudem unpacks here, the Bible actually affirms that borders are legitimate and walls are good things. God Himself scattered people by language (Gen. 11), and the promised land of Israel had definite borders, as did its surrounding nations. In fact, Moses respected the border of Edom by asking permission of the King of Edom to pass through that country (Moses was denied, as you'll read in Num. 20:17-21). Jesus acknowledged that nations need to be reached (Matt. 28:17-20), and Paul declared that God intends nations to have legitimate rulers (Rom. 13:1). Paul even used his status as a Roman citizen to protect himself from harm (Acts 22:25-26). And the Scriptural commands not to steal presuppose borders and the right to private property."

"(Remarkably, there will even be a border in the afterlife between heaven and hell because God can't force free creatures to love Him or one another. Forced love is impossible. Love requires freedom, and freedom requires the security that your choices will be respected, even if it means that you want an eternal border between you and God.)" (Turek, 2018).

This word of caution is presented on using the Old Testament verses as a defense for open border immigration. *"We must be careful when we quote the Bible in support of open borders. The Old Testament laws were written in the context of a theocracy. You can't pick and choose the laws from theocratic Israel and ignore the theocracy itself. Open borders are indeed biblical in a theocratic nation. If we lived in a Christian constitutional republic, open borders would be legitimate, as long as worshiping any other God but the Triune God of the Bible was outlawed. The United States by design is not a constitutional Christian republic, so arguments from Old Testament law for open borders are irrelevant."* (Ball, 2018).

As theologian Wayne Grudem, professor Phoenix Seminary, was quoted earlier, the following is part of an essay on the subject of Biblical walls done for Townhall electronic news in 2018. "In the world of the Old Testament, people built walls around cities to protect themselves from thieves, murderers, and other criminals, and from foreign invaders who would seek to destroy the city. People could still enter the city, but they had to do so by the gate, so that city officials would have some control over who was coming in and going out. Today's debate is about a larger area – a national border, not a city – but the principles are the same," Grudem explained."

"He added that Psalms 122, 147, and 51, all of which contain references to peace and security within walls or borders, further bolsters this notion. And after King David, Solomon completed and strengthened the wall around Jerusalem, he said."

"Yet when the Israelites turned away from God, the Babylonians broke down the walls, which indicated God's judgement against them and "as long as the wall around Jerusalem was broken down, it was a mark of shame and derision," the theologian wrote, referencing Nehemiah 1:3."

"The pathetic shame of a city without walls is also evident in this proverb: 'A man without self-control is like a city broken into and left without walls' (Proverbs 25:28). The implication is that such a man and such a city are both headed for destruction."

In addition, the Jews rebuilt the wall around Jerusalem when they returned from Babylonian captivity, and in Revelation 21 the Apostle John saw a wall surrounding the New Jerusalem in a vision, he said." (Grudem, 2018).

Adding to the discussion is the term "just war thinking". This eludes to a type of Christian war necessary to protect those within a border. Not all in need or suffering are immigrants attempting to enter the United States and whom so much Biblical scripture is recited to support their effort but there are also needy and suffering people within the United States' borders that also need to be protected foreign trespassers. This is the just war tradition of Christianity. John Shelton works in the U. S. Congress covering policy issues. A synopsis of his remarks follows: "Using the logic of the just war tradition, I want to make a specifically Christian case for securing our borders: constrained by the bounds of just war thinking, securing our borders can be an instance of Christian enemy love. To make this argument, I will proceed by *summarizing* the Christian core of the just war tradition, *apply its principles* to our border security debates, *draw out several policy implications* for Christians to mull over, and *conclude with some further reflections on thinking with tradition*, particularly the just war tradition. In this brief outline of the tradition's core, we can already begin to see the way in which the Christian duty to love the neighbor and the enemy could guide a basis for walls and border security. We can imagine how walls and border security might prevent thieves from having ever set upon the Good Samaritan's patient in the first place and how this could constitute an act of love. But what if the Good Samaritan's patient were an immigrant outside the walls? Those protected by border security may be Americans *as well as* immigrants." (Shelton, 2019).

Compassion, Borders, Nations

With the continuation of the Good Samaritan and immigrant dialog, one should consider the bigger picture that is evolving. That is the push towards liberalization of the political landscape and how intersectionality is at the core of that mission. Columnist David Limbaugh summarized liberal compassion that is major plank in their platform and intersectionality as such: "But beyond the superficial rhetoric, liberalism does not stand the test of compassion, because it subordinates individuality to identity groups and the collective and degrades human dignity. One of the great ironies of secular humanism is its purported championship of mankind as the measure of all things while undermining what makes us human.

How can a philosophy that devalues human individuality ultimately be compassionate toward human beings?"

"The latest rage is intersectionality, which establishes new hierarchies of victimhood and privilege based on the overlapping and interrelated categories of disadvantages that groups of people have experienced. We must no longer look at discrimination through the "single-axis framework" of race, gender, class, disability, etc., but understand how the various identities intersect. Some people have multiple "burdens" or "disadvantages," such that black women, for example, suffer more discrimination than black men and white women. Unless we refine our thinking to account for these combinations of disabilities, the most disadvantaged will be ignored. Isn't this exhausting? Who really thinks like this if not forced to?"

"Among other things, intersectionality is dehumanizing because people are demonized or protected depending on their group, not on what they have done or what they have personally experienced. How can people not see that this kind of thinking violates our basic sense of justice and accountability? Intersectionality, perhaps even more than the rudimentary forms of identity politics that preceded it, is also damaging to people because it forces them to focus on themselves as victims of disadvantaged groups rather than encourage them to strive, as individuals, to be the best they can be." (Limbaugh, 2019).

Liberalism pushes for universal government that is compassionate in that it gives people what the governing want people to have and categorizes of people into groups who receive universal benefits based upon which group they are in. To accomplish this, the system needs immigration to confuse the sovereignty of a nation and one way to accomplish that is to use Biblical Scripture falsely to alter people's beliefs. That is why a factual understanding of what the Bible says about immigration, nations and borders is necessary. For clarity of the Bible's directive on nations and immigrant status, the following lengthy description is recommended for a responsible counter to open borders and unlimited immigration when Scripture such as Matthew 25 is used. There are equal numbers of Scriptures on how and why God laid out borders and nations and different languages. A review of Genesis 11:6-8 and Babel explains this. For now, an understanding of the Biblical classification of inhabitants within a nation and their rights and privileges thereof.

"In numerous OT (Old Testament) passages, the student of Scripture learns that the God of Israel distinguished among three types of people in the land; those are summarized in the following sidebar.

Citizen	**Countryman**	*Ach*
Legal Immigrant	**Sojourner**	*Ger/Toshab*
Foreigner	**Illegal**	*Nokri/Zar*

The above are important biblical monikers of distinction that God makes relative to people in a given country. An Israelite citizen is referred to as a ***countryman*** (*ach*) in Scripture, whereas a legal immigrant is referred to as a ***sojourner*** (*ger*) or *toshab*, and a foreigner is called an ***illegal*** (*nokri*) or *zar*. Important to this study, and evident from the OT, is that an ***illegal*** did not possess the same benefits or privileges as a ***sojourner*** or ***countryman***. This fact can be illustrated from many passages. Notice, for instance, the words of Ruth the Moabite and her response to Boaz the Israelite in Ruth 2:10: ***Then she fell on her face, bowing to the ground and said to him, "Why have I found favor in your sight that you should take notice of me, since I am a foreigner?"***

"Not only was Ruth a ***foreigner*** (*nokri*), an ***illegal*** immigrant, she was a Moabite ***illegal***, who according to Deuteronomy 23:3 was forbidden to migrate into Israel altogether! For **Citizen** Boaz to entertain Ruth at all was remarkably generous and gracious, and possibly even against the law of the land. (Perhaps Boaz already had in mind legitimizing her status by marriage.) The point is that Ruth's self-declaration serves to underscore the classification of people in and by ancient Israel."

"Furthermore, a ***citizen/countryman*** was expressly forbidden to take advantage of or mistreat a ***legal immigrant***, known as a ***sojourner***, per Exodus 22:21 and Deuteronomy 10:19 respectively:

__"You shall not wrong a sojourner or oppress him, for you were sojourners in the land of Egypt (ESV)."__

__Love the sojourner, therefore, for you were sojourners in the land of Egypt__ *(ESV).*

Informing an immigration theology, a ***sojourner*** could be likened to a ***legal immigrant*** and a ***foreigner*** could be likened to an ***illegal immigrant*** today. Note Hoffmeier, a biblical expert on this subject: A sojourner (sometimes translated as stranger) was a person who entered Israel and followed legal procedures to obtain recognized standing as a resident alien." Hoffmeier goes on to say, that on the other hand, Israel treated ***illegal immigrants*** differently: Illegal immigrants should not expect these same privileges from the state whose laws they disregard by virtue of their undocumented status. These standard categories of one's standing in a given nation, and the differentiation between ***citizens, immigrants,*** and ***foreigners*** are representative of the will of God. In fact, these categorizations have been the distinctions in the mind of God ever since He scattered the people into different nations in Genesis 11. Further, the classification of people today in most every nation is based on Israel's OT example." (Drollinger, 2019).

The following provides some imperatives on borders and nations from a Biblical perspective. Exodus 23:31 "I will fix your boundary from the Red Sea to the sea of the Philistines, and from the wilderness to the River Euphrates; for I will deliver the inhabitants of the land into your hand, and you will drive them out before you."

Acts 17:26 "…and He made from one man every nation of mankind to live on all the face of the earth, having determined their appointed times and the boundaries of their habitation,"

Deuteronomy 32:8 "When the Most High gave the nations their inheritance, When He separated the sons of man, He set the boundaries of the peoples According to the number of the sons of Israel."

Nehemiah 9:22 "You also gave them kingdoms and peoples and allotted them to them as a boundary. They took possession of the land of Sihon the king of Heshbon and the land of Og the king of Bashan."

Psalm 74:17 "You have established all the boundaries of the earth; You have made summer and winter."

Proverbs 15:25 "The LORD will tear down the house of the proud, But He will establish the boundary of the widow."

Exodus 34:24 "For I will drive out nations before you and enlarge your borders, and no man shall covet your land when you go up three times a year to appear before the LORD your God."

Joshua 15 uses the word "boundary" 15 times in describing the nation of Judea. Detail must have been the order of the day when God laid out His idea of national divisions. Not only detailing boundaries but also who should live within them. "The Scriptures make it clear that national sovereignty, including clearly defined borders, is God's idea. In Acts 17:26, we read, "And he made from one man every nation of mankind to live on all the face of the earth, having determined allotted periods and the boundaries of their dwelling place..."

"Two things, we are told, are under God's sovereign control: how long a nation lasts, and where its borders are. The verb translated "having determined" is the Greek verb "horizo," from which we get the word "horizon." It means "to mark out, to define." So, God has marked out and defined the borders of each country. Our southern border is there by God's design. To disregard it, to treat it as if it were not there, to regard it as something not worth respecting and defending, is an insult to the God who put it there for our benefit." (Fischer, 2014).

Fischer more recently in January 2019 discussed borders and Matthew 25 regarding some evangelical comments supporting unlimited immigration based upon the Scripture. "Evangelicals, on the other hand, in line with the Word of God, recognize national sovereignty marked by borders, and recognize borders as God's idea, based on Acts 17:26. The EIT (Evangelical

Immigration Table), on the other hand, is for immigration without restriction regardless of national borders, and regardless of the impact of uncontrolled immigration on the spiritual and moral character of the United States. That's not evangelicalism, that's socialism."

"Russell Moore and the EIT bring their socialist interpretation to the biblical passage which is the centerpiece of their propaganda, Matthew 25:31-46. This is the parable in which people are admitted by God into his eternal kingdom based on whether they fed the hungry, gave drink to the thirsty, welcomed the stranger, clothed the naked and visited the sick and those in prison."

"Socialist evangelicals such as Moore misinterpret and misapply this passage right out of the box, for they treat it as if the parable was spoken to government. It's not. Governments don't go into the eternal kingdom- people do. So, the parable in Matthew 25 is spoken to us as individual followers of Jesus Christ. It's not the government's job to do any of those things, it's up to us as members of the body of Christ. And in my experience, the church and the Christians within do all these things. Churches I have pastored or belonged to have stocked food banks to help the hungry, collected warm winter coats to help clothe the needy in the winter months, have engaged in prison ministries to visit inmates and have consistently visited the sick in the hospital." (Fischer, Russell Moore Mangles Matthew 25, 2019).

Matthew 25 is a Biblical directive to Christians as individuals. Romans 13, specifically verses 1-7, is a Biblical directive to government. As individuals, we are to have compassion on the less fortunate, care for the needy, elderly, and widowed and refugee. The role of government is to preserve order, protect citizens, and punish wrongdoers.

The individual mandate of Matthew 25 has been covered earlier in this chapter and covered a variety of opinions as to its implications. The role of government should have equal coverage since it is important that the Scriptures are used in context as to whom directed and what the message actually is. Scripture says that governments are also God's creation and part of His plan. Therefore, Christians should respect governments and the rule of law they have established. Romans 13 explains that those in authority are God's servants. Good will be rewarded, evil will be condemned. Verses 1-7 are provided: "Let every person be subject to the governing authorities. For there is no authority except from God, and those that exist have been instituted by God. Therefore, whoever resists the authorities resists what God has appointed, and those who resist will incur judgment. For rulers are not a terror to good conduct, but too bad. Would you have no fear of the one who is in authority? Then do what is good, and you will receive his approval, for he is God's servant for your good. But if you do wrong, be afraid, for he does not bear the sword in vain. For he is the servant of God, an avenger who carries out God's wrath on the wrongdoer. Therefore, one must be in subjection, not only to avoid God's wrath but also for the sake of conscience. For because of this you also pay taxes, for the authorities are ministers of God, attending to this very thing. Pay to all what is owed to them: taxes to whom taxes are owed, revenue to whom revenue is owed, respect to whom respect is owed, honor to whom honor is owed."

Of note is the authority of God delegates to civil government to provide justice and not mercy. Mercy is the domain of the individual. Old Testament Scripture that is often used to advocate for open borders is Leviticus 19:33-34. Referring again to the definitions of individuals listed above, Leviticus refers to the temporary traveler passing through. It is expected that this traveler respects the laws of the land through which they are traveling. Illegal immigrants are often found not respecting the law of the land nor is it their intention to simply be passing through the country. The condemnation here is not directed at the immigrant but at the misuse of Scripture to advocate for a political accomplishment. This paragraph from the Center of Immigration Studies is germane. "Nor is it reasonable to jump to the conclusions many on the open borders side do about related passages. These activists claim that such passages mandate that a society welcome any and all foreigners presenting themselves. No such passages state or imply overlooking illegality committed on the part of the alien in his entry. Nor is there any requirement of unlimited or uncontrolled admittance of those who are members of another nation or society. Assertions like those are, at a minimum, a wrong reading. Such verses actually indicate nothing about the grounds for alien admission to ancient Israel." (John R. Edwards, 2009).

The Center for Immigration Studies further provides a good reference on the understanding of Scripture directives and the difference obligations under justice and under mercy. Their excerpt states: "Believers have long grasped the instruction of passages such as Micah 6:8: "He has told you, O man, what is good; and what does the Lord require of you but to do justice, and to love kindness, and to walk humbly with your God?" Some translations use the word "mercy" instead of "kindness." American University Professor Daniel Driesbach has found Micah 6:8 to rank among the most cited scriptures by America's founding generation.

Justice and mercy, along with a godly life, are fundamental principles of biblical conduct. Justice and mercy are complementary principles. They informed the thoughts of America's Founders as they fashioned a government for the new nation.

Government's wielding of the sword of justice is well established, biblically, as discussed earlier. Jesus did not challenge that principle, either toward Rome or other earthly authorities, nor did He question the legitimacy of civil (or religious) government.

Government's exercise of mercy is more challenging than its role in ensuring justice. Examples of mercy in public policy exist; for instance, granting a criminal a pardon or parole before he serves out his prison sentence, having proportionality for punishment of a crime (e.g., an eye for an eye, rather than a life for an eye). But most such policies aim in a rifle-shot fashion at individual cases, and often they involve some level of merit. U.S. immigration statutes have provided for suspending deportation in certain exceptional hardship cases. The adverse effects of not carrying out the justice due against guilty individuals are reduced somewhat by these acts' limited scope and infrequent application." (John R. Edwards, 2009).

Luke 6:36 also provides another individual directive saying "Be ye therefore merciful, as your Father is also merciful". If public policy were to force a population to apply the personal mandates from either the Old Testament or the New Testament, such acts of compassion, mercy, and acceptance would be done under duress and compulsion and would hardly be mercy or love. Also, God judges nations on righteousness on earth since nations will not be judged in Heaven. Only individuals will ascend to eternal life.

A final word from the Center of Immigration Studies article fittingly characterizes the dilemma of amnesty to illegal immigrants. "A compassionate act, when exercised by an individual, often becomes an injustice when compelled by civil government — the agents who are supposed to be the guardians of justice and protectors of the innocent, "the least of these," the citizens or subjects of their jurisdiction. Thus, for example, writing into the U.S. Constitution a prohibition against cruel punishment (e.g., torture, which European governments had instituted, such as in the Spanish Inquisition or the English Star Chamber) is an appropriate adaptation of the biblical standards of mercy; freeing thieves and batterers from facing imprisonment, restitution, and accountability to society is inappropriate and not merciful."

"How might this concept apply in U.S. immigration policy? Take amnesty, for example. Forgiving foreigners for entering the country illegally or staying when their visas expire might be seen as "merciful" or "compassionate," at least in its effect on the people gaining legal status without having to suffer the consequences the law otherwise would require of them. However, the government, as agent, has acted in such a way that coerces innocent citizens and law-abiding immigrants to suffer the consequences." (John R. Edwards, 2009).

PRIDE AND SPIRITUAL STRUGGLES

It's All About Pride

The Mueller report on Russian interference in the 2016 Presidential election was handed to the Attorney General on Friday, March 22. After an internal Department of Justice review, a four-page summary was released to the public. As anyone following even the smallest amount of media news was aware, the special counsel investigation divided the country into two camps. Those wishing to see the President charged with some crime and those supporting the President. For over two years, the main street media had been about 90% hoping for indictments and the minority trying to stay factual about the investigation. Since the findings announced no indictments and no collusion with the Russians, the ratings/viewership for CNN and MSNBC dropped 30% and 20% respectively overnight. Americans now seem bored with the constant bombardment of Russian collusion and perhaps feel let down by a media that every night kept telling them that something big was there.

The politicians that had pushed the same type of narrative as the media are now grasping at new accusations to keep from appearing as misleading as the media. No one is giving up. If Plan A, Mueller investigation, didn't work then surely Plan B, whatever that may be, will work. The strange but typical human behavior that has been and continues to unfold before the American public's eye is a textbook example of pride that captivates a body and won't let go. From a Biblical perspective there is ample Scripture about letting pride consume one's life. Perhaps it is not too much of a stretch to see that the exhibition of pride being witnessed so publicly today by certain media establishments and politicians relates to a spiritual struggle. Those wishing for the demise of the Presidency feel let down and are struggling to come to grasp with such a deflation of expectations. Christians know this feeling since spiritual struggle is much the same experience. Christians struggle to maintain the high experienced at first finding Christ. Over time the high wears off and doubt sets in. Christians regroup and get reinvigorated knowing that their travel in this life is a marathon and it will have its ups and downs. It is going to be interesting to observe how damaging pride will be for those unwilling to abandon their pride and move on. The remedy for those suffering from an excess amount of pride is what Christians employ when they are struggling spiritually.

It is important to step back and remember the nine fruits (sometimes expanded to 12) of the Holy Spirit because several of them are the antidote for excessive pride. The nine fruits referenced in Galatians 5:22-23 are love, joy, peace, forbearance, kindness, goodness, faithfulness, gentleness and self-control. The King James Version uses the word long-suffering instead of forbearance and gentleness instead of kindness. The King James Version uses long-suffering to impress patience. God operates on a different time schedule than our fast-paced lifestyles. His remedy to issues we classify as immediate are not so immediate on God's schedule. Gentleness is also more appropriate than kindness. Gentleness describes a behavior and a method of action that can be applied in multiple situations whereas kindness slants more towards benevolence. Gentleness can be applied in all situations and kindness is akin to a singular action.

Long-suffering and gentleness are two attributes that are stifled by pride. It can be said all of the nine fruits are displaced by pride to some degree. Long-suffering, hereafter called patience, is in short supply when one's pride has been damaged. Those of misplaced pride are competitive and want to win. When they don't win, they grow impatient for a resolution that once again, somehow, puts them back on top. What they overlook is that ultimately God judges truth and on God's timetable truth will be brought out. They lose patience because they can't overcome the truth. It mimics a spiritual struggle where the Christian is frustrated by occasional setbacks and confused about their spirituality. Christians accept that frustration and confusion are teachable moments since their focus is on the long term or end game and not just the immediate.

One way of avoiding having to confront such a catastrophic dose of pride would have been to apply the fruit of gentleness from the beginning. If one approaches an endurance race with full throttle at the beginning, there is no reserve for the final push. However, if the race is begun with a gentle pace, there is a reserve for the finish. So many began the collusion push full speed and tried to sustain that narrative for over two years. When the checkered flag was waved their pride had taken all of their energy and there was nothing left for the last lap. Had they only considered these two pieces of Scripture: King James Version Proverbs, 16:18, "Pride goeth before destruction, and a haughty spirit before a fall" and James 4:6 (KJV): "But he giveth more grace. Wherefore he saith, God resisteth the proud, but giveth grace unto the humble". One's approach or beginning often determines the outcome or ending.

With the backdrop of the recent political and investigative happenings, the parallel of spiritual struggling and pride will be examined independently.

Pride

Before beginning the review of the negative aspects of harmful pride, two studies will provide some balance on the subject. The first is a longitudinal study of older English people. This study addresses the value of positive pride, having pride in your appearance and social graces. The second addresses the use of the word "pride" and "arrogance" in the Bible. Proverbs 16:18-19 should be read to properly delineate between the effect of pride and the effect of haughty. "Pride goeth before destruction, and an haughty spirit before a fall. Better it is to be of an humble spirit with the lowly, than to divide the spoil with the proud." Proverbs 16:18-19, KJV.

"Results: The findings did not support the contention that "pride comes before a fall." Unadjusted estimates indicate that the odds of reported falls were significantly lower for people with high pride levels compared with those who had low pride (odds ratio 0.69, 95% confidence interval

0.58 to 0.81, P<0.001). This association remained after adjustment for age, sex, household wealth, and history of falls (odds ratio 0.81, 0.68 to 0.97, P<0.05). It was partially attenuated after further adjustment for mobility problems, eyesight problems, the presence of a limiting long-term illness, a diagnosis of arthritis or osteoporosis, medication use, cognitive function, and pain and depression (odds ratio 0.86, 0.72 to 1.03, P<0.1). Because the confidence interval exceeded 1 in the final model, it remains possible that pride may not be an independent predictor of falls when known risk factors are considered. People with moderate pride did not have lower odds of having fallen than those with low pride in adjusted models. Participants lost to follow-up did not differ from those retained in terms of key variables and weighting the analyses to account for selective attrition did not produce different results."

"Conclusions contrary to the well-known saying "pride comes before a fall," these findings suggest that pride may actually be a protective factor against falling in older adults. Future studies may seek to investigate the mechanisms underpinning this relation." (D McMinn, 2017).

"While pride is sometimes used in the Old Testament in a positive sense (i.e., the "pride" of the land of Israel [Psalm 47:4 ; Ezek 24:21] or, God's "pride/majesty/excellency" [Exod 15:7 ; Job 37:4 ; Isa 2:10]), its negative sense predominates, occurring in sixty-one texts. "Pride" is found mainly in the prophets and the books of poetry." (Dunnett, 2019).

Some observations on pride are too good to not be repeated as originally written. These few paragraphs by Thomas Tarrants, Vice President of the C. S. Lewis Institute, sum up some of our modern-day infatuation with self-centered pride. Let us recall the antidote of humility. "C.S. Lewis, another top contender for having had the greatest impact for Christ in the twentieth century, called pride "the great sin." Every believer should read his chapter by that title in Mere Christianity. There Lewis said,

According to Christian teachers, the essential vice, the utmost evil, is Pride. Unchastity, anger, greed, drunkenness, and all that, are mere flea bites in

comparison: it was through Pride that the devil became the devil: Pride leads to every other vice: it is the complete anti-God state of mind…

… it is Pride which has been the chief cause of misery in every nation and every family since the world began.[1]

If this sounds like exaggeration, it will help us to know that Lewis is not simply giving us his private opinion but summarizing the thinking of great saints through the ages. Augustine and Aquinas both taught that pride was the root of sin.[2] Likewise Calvin, Luther, and many others. Make no mistake about it: pride is the great sin. It is the devil's most effective and destructive tool."

"I encourage you to read and meditate on Uzziah's full story in 2 Chronicles 26. The stories of Haman (Esther 3–7) and Nebuchadnezzar (Daniel 4) also offer valuable insights into pride and are well worth reading. This is evident today in the dangerous pride in some political and business leaders in the West. We have only to look around us at the current state of political life in America to see examples. Pride and arrogance are obvious in many political leaders, whether liberal or conservative, making matters much worse than they need to be. Or consider the business and financial catastrophes we have experienced in recent years. A thoughtful article in the Wall Street Journal after the WorldCom and Enron debacles attributed them to "pride, greed and lack of accountability." The recent financial crisis in America is yet another example of the same thing. Clearly pride is very dangerous and can produce widespread suffering in society when people in leadership and power are corrupted by it." (Thomas A. Tarrants, 2011).

A few selected Scriptures that are mostly in Proverbs clearly lays out the case that pride is a human quality with a fairly high undesirability rating. The offsetting quality garnered from these verses is again humility. The everyday situations as seen on television or read from news sources can quickly been linked to pride standing in the way of what should be more reasoned talk from people privileged to have a national audience. One can tell by the tenseness in the voices of those on television that they are having a difficult time letting go of their obsession and the mantle of pride is hanging dreadfully around their neck. These verses address the outcome of too much pride and its eventual ramification.

"The wicked, through the pride of his countenance, will not seek after God: God is not in all his thoughts."
Psalms 10:4, KJV

"The fear of the LORD is to hate evil: pride, and arrogancy, and the evil way, and the froward mouth, do I hate."
Proverbs 8:13, KJV

"When pride cometh, then cometh shame: but with the lowly is wisdom."
Proverbs 11:2, KJV

"Only by pride cometh contention: but with the well advised is wisdom."
Proverbs 13:10, KJV

"In the mouth of the foolish is a rod of pride: but the lips of the wise shall preserve them."
Proverbs 14:3, KJV

"The fear of the LORD is the instruction of wisdom; and before honour is humility."
Proverbs 15:33, KJV

"Pride goeth before destruction, and an haughty spirit before a fall. Better it is to be of an humble spirit with the lowly, than to divide the spoil with the proud."
Proverbs 16:18-19, KJV

"A man's pride shall bring him low: but honour shall uphold the humble in spirit."
Proverbs 29:23, KJV

Michael Bradley's piece in Bibleknowledge.com had some less than flattering observations about pride and its abandonment in sanctification. He has some startling conclusions about pride later in the paragraph presented here. "As part of the sanctification process that God would like to start with each one of us – one of the first things that God will be doing, through the power of the Holy Spirit, is to either take out or prevent certain types of negative qualities from entering into our personalities. Without question, one of the major negative qualities that God will be moving very strongly on to either prevent it from being able to enter into us to any significant degree, or to literally knock it right out of us if it has moved too far up into our personalities, is the negative quality of pride. This cancerous, lethal, and destructive quality, probably more than any other negative quality, has brought down more kingdoms, toppled more empires, caused more wars, destroyed more marriages, ruined more friendships, and led more criminals into our jail systems than all of the other negative qualities combined and put together." (Bradley, 2018). It is being consumed in pride that creates the negative impact. Certain levels of pride are positive. Like many things, the same attribute can be good and bad, misused or managed. Some other definitions for pride, including the dictionary, show the direction of acceptable pride. They are: Proper respect for one-self, self-respect, a reasonable or justifiable self-respect, sense of one's own dignity and self-worth, and delight or satisfaction in one's own or another's achievements.

Webster's dictionary has a longer list of negative attributes attached to pride than positive attributes: An unduly high opinion of oneself, exaggerated self-esteem, conceit, haughty behavior resulting from arrogance, an improper and excessive self-esteem known as conceit and arrogance, a sin of attitude and of the heart and spirit, a puffed up and inflated ego, boasting and high-mindedness, a conceited sense of one's superiority, highly exalted in attitude, opposite from the virtue of humility.

From both the dictionary's definition, you can see many aspects of the explanation of pride used in Scripture. How closely the antidote of humility is associated with the negative aspect of pride is pronounced. The word "haughty" is also mentioned in the same Scriptures and addresses the physical characteristics associated with pride and the signs that are very visible when pride is in control. These definitions show the bond haughty has to pride showing great pride on oneself; disdain, contempt or scorn for others; proud, arrogant, supercilious (disdain or contemptuous), and an arrogant spirit.

Pride has the distinction of being among the seven deadly sins whose origin is in Christian theology. They are pride, envy, gluttony, greed, lust, sloth, and wrath. Their counterpart for clarity is the seven heavenly virtues: humility (pride), kindness (envy), temperance (gluttony), charity (greed), chastity (lust), diligence (sloth), and patience (wrath).

"The sin of pride is the sin of sins. It was this sin, we're told, which transformed Lucifer, an anointed cherub of God, the very "seal of perfection, full of wisdom and perfect in beauty," into Satan, the devil, the father of lies, the one for whom Hell itself was created. We're warned to guard our hearts against pride lest we too "fall into the same condemnation as the devil." St. Augustine of Hippo (354-430 A.D.) wrote, "'Pride is the commencement of all sin'[6] because it was this which overthrew the devil, from whom arose the origin of sin; and afterwards, when his malice and envy pursued man, who was yet standing in his uprightness, it subverted him in the same way in which he himself fell. The sin of pride is a preoccupation with self. God despises the sin of pride especially because it's totally contrary to His purposes for us. He wants us to live by His example and to serve each other in love. And He's given us the most beautiful example. Not only did He die for us, He lives for us as well." (Sin Of Pride, 2019).

Struggling Faith or Struggling Pride

How do we regain our faith and put our pride aside? Is there ground for releasing one while building up the other? "Pride is a prison that perpetuates anger, hurt, and foolishness while keeping at bay the restorative effects of conviction, humility, and reconciliation (Proverbs 11:2; 29:23; Galatians 6:3; James 4:6; Revelation 3:17–20). Later, in Proverbs 16:18, God tells us, "Pride goes before destruction, and a haughty spirit before a fall." Not only would pride be your jailer, but it would also be your executioner. Compare this reaction to our Lord and Savior Jesus Christ. If ever there was one who had the right for his pride to be as big as life, it was the one through whom all life came into being. If Jesus had come into the world and demanded that all serve him, and do so immediately, it would not have been arrogant; it would have been appropriate. Yet as Philippians 2 tells us, he came not in the form of a ruler but a servant." (Squires, 2015).

Prison, perpetuates anger, hurt and foolishness; all are descriptors of pride. Not a pleasant way to be defined. Jesus came to be among His people as a servant to them. His life was one of being humble. Those struggling with their faith and letting pride be a limiter on their regaining their pride should let the Holy Spirit enable their spirit and regain their Jesus-centered humility. Today's political environment is playing out in front of us the very despicable symptoms of pride. Not being able to let something go is a disease that eats away at your ability to enjoy and appreciate the day you have been given. Not only is your day gone but your days ahead will not be any more enjoyable either.

The symptoms of pride impact your faith. Fear is a symptom. Its implications are real. "We fear because we don't have faith in the Lord, we are enormously preoccupied with ourselves, and we don't have control." (Crow, 2017). Matthew 14:31 is a premier reference for faith. Entitlement is embedded in pride while self-sacrifice is within the humble heart. Romans 3:23 and 6:23 address clearly that we are entitled to nothing and our sins are punishable. Luke 22:26 reminds us again that it is about serving rather than living to receive accolades for how great we are.

By focusing on ourselves we are in a constant state of ingratitude for what we do have. We have an inflated idea about what we deserve rather than focusing how much have we given today. Numerous Scriptures speak that by giving we get more, Deuteronomy 2:7 and Psalm34:9. God, through the Holy Spirit, is not going to enter your heart is you don't invite Him in. The rule of the world unseen by us is that the Holy Spirit, the enabler, will not go where not invited. Living in a world that only evaluates what we don't have can be changed to one that sees what blessings we do have by simply opening the heart to let God in. If pride is self-worshipping and self-preservation above all, then as much as you desire to please people you will fail. "The apostle Paul knew human approval was a pointless and prideful pursuit. Because of that, he could say, "For am I now seeking the approval of man, or of God? Or am I trying to please man? If I were still trying to please man, I would not be a servant of Christ" (Galatians 1:10)." (Crow, 2017).

Prayer is the pathway to regaining your faith and overcoming selfish pride. Avoid hypocrisy by speaking and judging in one way while living another. Do not continue to rebel against something that you know is right, but you insist on knowing better. It is because of Jesus' humility that we are capable of being forgiven, even from our overzealous pride.

Eliminate Pride, Strengthen Spirituality

These verses set the stage for eliminating hurtful pride from our lives and regain our spiritual strength. Numbers 12:3-Moses was very meek, above all men on face of the earth and Matthew 11:29,30-Jesus said, "I am meek and lowly in heart." The following verses closely parallel the previous two. Matthew 5:5-Blessed are the meek (gentle-NKJV), for they shall inherit the earth. Jesus declares a "blessing" (happiness) on those who are meek and Galatians 5:22,23-Meekness is one of the fruits of the Spirit-qualities that we must possess if we are led by the Spirit. These short verses remind us of the example Jesus put before us and the virtue, if not reward, of a humble life.

Meekness is not a behavior of weakness. As discovered in 1 Peter 3:4, meekness is about an attitude or quality of the heart. Humility is an attitude or quality of the mind as extrapolated from Acts 20:19. Both meekness and humility are directed towards our reverence to God to whom we must be both meek and humble. We are not righteous but only self-righteous. The word "haughty" should be a caution light to us in this regard.

Correct All by Calling "In the Name of Jesus"

A starting point for corrective action for harmful pride is to recall the power of Jesus's name. If you are struggling with your spiritual conviction because pride has a hold on your vision of the world, remember that your anchor should always be to seek your solution by calling on Jesus. These verses are helpful reminders of that power.

There is no other name under heaven given among men by which we must be saved. – Acts 4:12

At the name of Jesus every knee should bow. – Philippians 2:10

You were washed, you were sanctified, you were justified in the name of the Lord Jesus Christ. – 1 Corinthians 6:11

Whatever you ask in my name, this I will do. – John 14:13

Lord, even the demons are subject to us in your name! – Luke 10:17

Signs and wonders are performed through the name of your holy servant Jesus. – Acts 4:30

For everyone who calls on the name of the Lord will be saved. – Romans 10:13

The following is a synthesis of one of the most comforting verses in the Bible, John 16:23-24: "Praying in the name of Jesus is powerful because when we pray in His name, we pray with His authority. God promises to answer whatever we ask in His name according to His will. This is why we must know the will of God in order to pray with the authority of Jesus. This truth is wonderful because we have the assurance that He hears our prayers. Through prayer in His name we shall make known among the nations what He has done. Have you taken advantage of this glorious promise in your own life circumstances? John 16:23-24 says: "In that day you will no longer ask me anything. Very truly I tell you, my Father will give you whatever you ask in my name. Until now you have not asked for anything in my name. Ask and you will receive, and your joy will be complete." (Przybylski, 2015).

It is the Name of Jesus that He left with us before His ascent into Heaven after the resurrection. It is a Name of authority and it was our key to open the door to communicate with God. "In My Name! In the Name of Jesus! He authorized us. He gave us His Name as the authority. The power is in the Name. The authority is in the Name. He gave us the Name that is above every name. He gave us the Name that is recognized in three worlds—the Name that has authority in heaven, on earth, and under the earth. Angels, men, and demons have to bow at that Name—and that Name belongs to us. We are authorized to use that Name." (Hagin, 2019).

"Any power attributed to the name of Jesus originates in the *Person* of Jesus. When we "believe in Jesus' name," we are trusting in the finished work of the risen Christ on the cross (1 John 5:13). *Jesus* is not a magic word. There is nothing special about the arrangement of the letters in His name. Had Jesus not been God in the flesh who lived a perfect life, died for the sins of all who would believe, and rose again, we wouldn't even be talking about His name. Any power that Christians access in Jesus' name comes from true faith in who Jesus is and what He does for sinners."

Calling upon the name of Jesus is powerful and has been a demonstrated power for some. First though we must understand that the words are not the power but Jesus who chooses to grace us with His blessing at a time of need. The following reminds us of the true power that is in the name of Jesus. "There is no magical power in the name of Jesus—there is only power in Jesus Christ, Himself. By simply calling out the name of "Jesus," one cannot expect a special power, outcome, or better standing with God. The name of Jesus is precious, however, and brimming with meaning. From Pastor Kevin DeYoung: "What about Jesus? 'And you shall call his name Jesus,' the angel told Joseph, 'for he will save his people from their sins' (Matt. 1:21). More than a great teacher, more than an enlightened man, more than a worker of miracles, more than a source of meaning in life, more than a self-help guru, more than a self-esteem builder, more than a political liberator, more than a caring friend, more than a transformer of cultures, more than a purpose for the purposeless, Jesus is the Savior of sinners." (Is there power in the name of Jesus?, 2019).

There is an open invitation to call upon Jesus directly by using His name. "First, that we recognize the power of the name of Jesus and invoke it for our own benefit and for that of others. It is clear from the Gospels that the Name of Jesus holds extraordinary power. In his Name, demons are cast out and the sick are healed. And we are invited in the Gospels to use this Name for our own benefit and for that of others. Those who invoke this name draw upon this power. "if you ask anything in my Name, I will do it." Orthodox Bishop Kallistos Ware explains that "God's name is essentially linked with His Person, and so the Invocation of the divine Name possesses a genuinely sacramental character, serving as an effective sign of (God's) invisible presence and action. For the believing Christian today, as in apostolic times, the Name of Jesus is power."](Vryhof, 2017).

The conclusion must be that pride is an active issue with much of political discourse openly demonstrating nothing but pride as an obstacle to agreement. With such bombardment of resentment towards Christians and so many other groups of people, it is little wonder that the Christian community is feeling like their spirit and faith are lessening. In reality, only the imaginative world is changing. If you hear the same message for so long and from so many, it is normal that you begin to have doubts about your beliefs and convictions. The tactic is one of wearing you down. If a lie is continually perpetuated and is repeated by so many, it becomes real without any evidence. The reason that people and groups resist accepting another point of view or belief is their pride will not let them. They may know they are in the wrong, so to speak, but pride will make them resort to many different alliterations of their story to keep from accepting the truth. The subject of truth is worthy of its own discussion.

Pride is usually a bad factor. Humility is the antidote. Struggling spiritually is almost inevitable in the social environment of today. The best countermeasure is to call upon the name of Jesus and the power will be there for recovery and reinvigoration of one's faith. It is a continuing battle that must not be forfeited to those yet to concede to the truth. The study for the truth is a story all of its own.

PERSECUTION

Passive and Active Persecution

The topics highlighted in this writing are only a few of the incidences that could be explored. The few to be presented here are a good summation of what is happening in America today. Certainly, Christianity is targeted not only here but elsewhere in the world. The burning of the Notre Dame cathedral in Paris April 16, 2019 highlighted the number of churches that had been vandalized in France in the last short while. The number exceeds a few hundred, 1,063 exactly in 2018 (Ellis, 2019). Part of the anti-Christian movement has its historical roots where Muslims and Christians have long had their differences. These Christian episodes are explainable historically, but the episodes of anti-conservatism are local. It is the anti-conservative movement that has brought Christianity into the fray. Christian views closely parallel those most widely held by conservatives and the two groups are often mixed synonymously in the media and in conversation.

Easter Sunday 2019 began with these headlines: "Easter Sunday explosions at multiple churches and hotels rock Sri Lanka, death toll rises past 200" (Louis Casiano, 2019). A follow up the next day had this addition to the story: "One of the alleged suicide bombers of the Sri Lanka attack that killed 290 people and injured many more left a video easily viewed on the internet, where he explained that anyone who disagrees with Muslims should be killed."

"Unconfirmed reports put Mohammed Zahran, the leader of National Thowheed Jamath at the church where the Easter Sunday bombing took place. A video posted by Imam Mohamad Tawhidi where Zahran is explaining that "Anyone who disagrees with Muslims should be killed." (Morse, 2019).

The latest count is 290 Christians killed and around 500 wounded in a direct attack on Christians by a Muslim faction. When the Bible says that Christians will be persecuted, it is a truth that unfortunately is a modern-day reality. The same is happening in Ethiopia as well as China.

It is not only on foreign soil that Christians face a degree of shunning. A lot has been made in the media about some American notables using the words "Easter Worshippers" rather than Christians to describe the casualties in Sri Lanka. This headline is local: "Obama, Clinton, Democrats Denounce Attacks on 'Easter Worshippers,' Not 'Christians'." (Pollak, 2019).

It was clear that a political party that has policies much in defiance of the Bible has coined a new term to describe a population that they have an almost blasphemy necessity to avoid calling Christian. They obviously develop these terms and communicate them around their circle so as to use the influence of repetition to implant a concept into the reading or listening audience. An example of how the term "Easter Worshippers" was disseminated is below. Please note that the word "worshiper" is misspelled in each Twitter. They each spelled it with two "P's".

"The attacks on tourists and Easter worshippers in Sri Lanka are an attack on humanity. On a day devoted to love, redemption, and renewal, we pray for the victims and stand with the people of Sri Lanka."

— Barack Obama (@BarackObama) April 21, 2019

"On this holy weekend for many faiths, we must stand united against hatred and violence. I'm praying for everyone affected by today's horrific attacks on Easter worshippers and travelers in Sri Lanka."

— Hillary Clinton (@HillaryClinton) April 21, 2019

"On a day of redemption and hope, the evil of these attacks on Easter worshippers and tourists in Sri Lanka is deeply saddening. My prayers today are with the dead and injured, and their families. May we find grace."

— Julián Castro (@JulianCastro) April 21, 2019

"Heartbreaking to learn about the attacks on tourists and Easter worshippers in Sri Lanka. Colorado stands with the people of Sri Lanka during this very tragic day and we grieve for those affected by these acts of violence."

— Jared Polis (@GovofCO) April 21, 2019

"I am deeply saddened over the horrific acts of violence against Easter worshippers and tourists in Sri Lanka. I send my deepest condolences to the victims and their families. We stand united with the people of Sri Lanka."

— Ami Bera, M.D. (@RepBera) April 21, 2019

"Yet Obama, Clinton, and other Democrats — including 2020 presidential contender Julián Castro — could not bring themselves to identify the victims of the attacks as "Christians," calling them "Easter worshippers" instead in eerily similar responses:" (Pollak, 2019)

The Sri Lanka story is still developing but prior to that was another type of attack. The example of the young Catholic boys standing on the Capitol square waiting on a bus were approached by a Native American and the scene immediately became the characterization of how Catholic (Christian) privileged white boys treat elderly Native Americans. The short video would make you think that the story that became most popular was indeed true. Then a longer version of the video was released and revealed that the Catholic students were being harassed by a group across the street from them and that the Native American in question actually moved into the bus waiting boys. The narrative made popular by the media was completely opposite to what actually transpired. This was an immediate Rorschach test for America. It is antidotally said that we humans see only 40% as reality and 60% what our brain wants us to see. That is to say that our subconscious is a significant driving force in creating in our minds what our eyes are actually seeing. We see what we want to see. Scott Rasmussen is founder and president of the Rasmussen Media Group. They did two series of polls shortly after the Capitol square episode became a viral media phenomenon. They're first poll found that 74% of liberal responders thought that the Covington High students behaved inappropriately while only 31% of conservatives did. Their poll on the how the national media handled the story found that 75% of conservatives thought the media behaved irresponsibly while only 31% of the liberals did. Remarkably, after some time Rasmussen polled the same questions again and found that even after the storyline generated by the short video was completely rebuked by the longer video of the event, the positions did not change. This is the alarming situation we face today. Positions are now hard and fast despite some of those positions being completely dispelled. The truth does not change the mind. One can see that the truth in the Bible will fall on many deft ears and the truth will be resisted ferociously. This quote from Scott Rasmussen's article in Townhall sums it up well: "Sadly, this is the state of American politics in the 21st century. Rather than reserving judgment until the facts are known, politically obsessed activists look only for symbols to see if someone is on their team or the other team. Once that's decided, nothing else matters. Additional information is then useful only if it helps make the case for their side." (Rasmussen, 2019). Not only is the state of American politics but also the state of evangelism for Christians.

On another front, Christianity or conservatism gets little correct press or media attention to at least provide the public with the full and complete story and not just a sound bite that serves to support the reporter's or media outlet's political stance. Believe nothing that you see or hear is becoming a standard precaution for both readers and viewers. An example stood out prominently at the March for Life march in January 2019. The liberal media reported and provided images saying the March for Life crowd was around 1,000. Well, it was around 1,000. Around 100,000. They didn't lie but they certainly tried to downplay the support the March for Life garnered by deceptively reporting the event. Depending on the January weather in Washington, D. C. and their featured speaker, the March has had years of over half a million participants in the march. The reporting and coverage of the March for Life demonstrates that even images (videos) cannot be trusted since they may be selectively taken to push a particular narrative and the written or spoken work must be taken with a grain of salt so to speak. This type of selective public media presents considerable roadblocks to getting the correct Christian message out. The media gives the impression that Christian values are waning in America and support is faltering when perhaps the opposite is true. Christians are too polite to engage in the back-alley tactics employed by others against Christians and their Biblical values.

The following example of pigeon-holing people or cherry-picking data requires that I get personal. As a 100% disabled veteran and two tour Vietnam veteran and a faculty member teaching life science courses, this story baffles me. As a scientist who understands scientific rigor and two tour veteran that has the opportunity to not only know a lot of veterans but can share in their experience, the news on this story shows intended research bias. In other words, you create a study that will give you the outcome you want rather than the other way around.

An article in Breakpoint captures the essence of using science to slip its way into religion. It says: "The study, entitled "<u>Biological and cognitive underpinnings of religious fundamentalism</u>," was published in the journal Neuropsychologia. In it, researchers went over the data from 119 Vietnam War veterans who were "specifically chosen because a large number of them had damage to brain areas suspected of playing a critical role in functions related to religious fundamentalism." Also found in the above journal was a recent published study with the title "Tweaking your brain with magnets makes you LESS religious: Magnetic pulses increase non-spiritual reasoning, study claims." Seems there's a lot of brain research into religious tendencies.

"Is your Spidey-sense going off here? It should be… The researchers weren't studying the brains of 119 random people looking to see what, if anything, they might find. No, they *assumed* that a particular kind of brain damage played a role in whether someone became a religious fundamentalist, and then went looking for evidence that confirmed those suspicions." (Rivera, 2019).

The next hundred pages could address the statistical significance of this work and the adherence to scientific rigor but that is boring. An article like this being presented under the pretense of being science may be useful in terms of posing an interesting hypothesis for future research, but it is no means was meant for that purpose. Its purpose was to promote the notion that Vietnam veterans are for the most part crazy and there's some type of brain damage in anyone who might hold strongly held religious beliefs. Pretty much captures a lot; patriotic and generally conservative veterans and devout Christians.

Another battle of name calling continues in today's news. It seems some people are authorities as to who is more Christian and who will get into Heaven. The first starts with a reporter stating emphatically that a previous minister and state governor will not get into Heaven. The story is as such: "American Urban Radio Networks White House correspondent April Ryan on Friday melted down after former Gov. Mike Huckabee (AR-R) blasted her for calling for the firing his daughter, White House press secretary Sarah Huckabee Sanders."

"Appearing Thursday on CNN's *Outfront*, Ryan, who also serves as a political analyst for the network, claimed Sanders had no "credibility left" after special counsel Robert Mueller's report was released."

"She outright lied, and the people, the American people, can't trust her. They can't trust what's said from the president's mouthpiece, spokesperson, from the people's house," April said, referencing Sanders' statements regarding the firing of FBI Director James Comey."

"When there is a lack of credibility there, you have to start and start lopping the heads off. It's 'Fire Me Thursday' or 'Fire Me Good Friday.' She needs to go," she added."

"Huckabee, tweeting about Ryan suggesting his daughter have her head "lopped off," asked of the reporter's remarks, "So liberals—is this okay? Does CNN have the integrity to deal w/ this incitement to murder?" (Caplan, 2019).

But much before this was the story of Lady Gaga announcing that she was much more Christian than Vice President Mike Pence. The stories keep unfolding that present a clear picture that Christians are under assault from many directions and under many pretenses of proclaiming who is the more righteous. The Biblical comparative is in John 1:9 "If we confess our sins, he is faithful and just to forgive us our sins and to cleanse us from all unrighteousness." Philippians 1:11 makes clear that righteousness comes from Jesus and is not something that we ourselves can produce. 2 Corinthians 5:21 speaks of how the Jesus took our sins so that we might be righteous before God.

This is an excellent summation of what righteousness is about from Got Questions. "Dictionaries define *righteousness* as "behavior that is morally justifiable or right." Such behavior is characterized by accepted standards of morality, justice, virtue, or uprightness. The Bible's standard of human righteousness is God's own perfection in every attribute, every attitude, every behavior, and every word. Thus, God's laws, as given in the Bible, both describe His own character and constitute the plumb line by which He measures human righteousness." (What is righteousness?, 2019).

A couple of more entries into the series of passive attacks on Christianity played out before our own Congress. The first was a Senator suggesting a judicial nominee was "too Christian" to be trusted with judicating the law. One report read like this: "This afternoon, during a confirmation hearing for 7th Circuit Court of Appeals nominee Amy Coney Barrett, Democratic senator Dianne Feinstein attacked the nominee for her Roman Catholic faith."

"Barrett is a law professor at the University of Notre Dame who has written about the role of religion in public life and delivered academic lectures to Christian legal groups. Drawing on some of these materials, Feinstein launched a thinly veiled attack on Barrett's Catholic faith, asserting that her religious views will prevent her from judging fairly."

"When you read your speeches, the conclusion one draws is that the dogma lives loudly within you," Feinstein said. "And that's of concern when you come to big issues that large numbers of people have fought for years in this country." Feinstein is clearly hinting here at the Supreme Court decision in *Roe v. Wade*, a ruling that Feinstein supports so vociferously that she has even called it a "super-precedent." (DeSanctis, 2017). Apparently, having a relationship with a Christian denomination or being Catholic stamps you with a "dogma" that will be with you forever in whatever you do.

A second such incidence had to do with one's association with a Catholic group with a long history of benevolence. This one was an attack on the Knights of Columbus. It reads as follows: "Two Democratic senators are scrutinizing a federal judicial nominee over his membership in the Knights of Columbus, drawing a stern rebuke from the Catholic organization."

"Sens. Kamala Harris, D-Calif., and Mazie Hirono, D-Hawaii, raised concerns about Omaha-based lawyer Brian Buescher's membership as part of the Senate Judiciary Committee's review of his nomination by President Trump to sit on the U.S. District Court in Nebraska, as first reported by the Catholic News Agency."

"In a series of questions sent to Buescher, Hirono asked whether his membership in the Knights of Columbus would prevent him from hearing cases "fairly and impartially" and, if confirmed, whether he would end his membership in the Roman Catholic charitable organization."

"The Knights of Columbus has taken a number of extreme positions," Hirono said in the questionnaire. "For example, it was reportedly one of the top contributors to California's Proposition 8 campaign to ban same-sex marriage." (O'Reilly, 2017).

INTERCESSORY PRAYER, PRAYING FOR GOD TO INTERCEDE

Definition

The preceding nine chapters have shown a country that is giving way to a culture of self-indulgence and self-satisfaction. As this may be the choice of some, it is not the choice of all. This seems to matter little since those who are choosing not to follow God's principles want the rest of us to be quite and disappear. It is a movement that wants to criminalize everything the Bible stands for and it's the Christians that are the enemy of state. Without doubt, the judicial system has over reached its Constitutional authority. Whenever has a District court made a national ruling? District court rulings apply only to their district and the ruling applies only to those involved in the court suit. Now it is a normal expectation that District courts are making rulings that apply nation-wide. The liberalization of some of the court rulings is beyond traditional case law and common understanding. They are passing judgement on subjects in complete defiance of the Constitution and case law. The 9th Circuit Court has had so many of their cases overturned by the Supreme Court that those justices need to return to school and not a liberal one at that.

So, it seems impossible for Christians to stem the flow towards liberalism and the "no moral restrictions" lifestyle. We Christians haven't banded together yet to call out the ultimate weapon all Christians have and that is prayer. Martin Luther once said: "Behold, you could repulse the devil and all his false suggestions by basing your prayer on these three things: God's command, His promise, and the manner and words Christ Himself taught." Let us not forget the power in simply saying "in the name of

Jesus". Christians have power and more of those in Christian leadership positions and those in the Christian media are calling on Christians to pray.

The kind of prayer we need to be making today is called an intercessory prayer. When the problem is too big for us to handled or influence individually, we need to call upon the Higher Power. CBN has an excellent and succinct definition for intercessory prayer.

"A family member faces a deadly disease. Your neighbor desperately needs Jesus but turns away every time you try to share Christ. A nation begins to crumble because its people follow their own evil ways. But what can you do?"

"Often, the problems we face seem too big for us. No matter how much we try, we cannot solve them on our own. It's times like these when we need to turn to the Lord in intercessory prayer."

"Intercession is prayer that pleads with God for your needs and the needs of others. But it is also much more than that. Intercession involves taking hold of God's will and refusing to let go until His will comes to pass."

"Intercession is warfare–the key to God's battle plan for our lives. But the battleground is not of this earth. The Bible says, "We are not fighting against humans. We are fighting against forces and authorities and against rulers of darkness and spiritual powers in the heavens above" (Eph. 6:12)."

"Intercessory prayer takes place in this spiritual world where the battles for our own lives, our families, our friends and our nation are won or lost." (What Is Intercessory Prayer?, 2019).

Intercessory prayer is positioned with the need for Christians to stand in the gap to prevent the wall from being breached. This chapter continues with our duty to patch the cracks in our Christian world so that the forces that wish to undermine it and eliminate it are stopped in their tracks at some point. A continuation of the subject in CBN.com shows the relationship between intercessory prayer and "standing in the gap". "Throughout the

Bible, God searched for those willing to fight the spiritual battle for their land. In Ezekiel, God says, "And I searched for a man among them who should build up the wall and stand in the gap before Me for the land, that I should not destroy it, but I found no one" (Ezek. 22:30, NASB)."

"Through intercession, you can take the offensive in the spiritual battle, building up your community, your nation and your world. As you follow God's call to rise up and take your place in the spiritual battle, God promises to "heal their land" (2 Chron. 7:14, NASB)." (What Is Intercessory Prayer?, 2019).

Intercessory prayer has multiple purposes beyond praying for national healing. So that it's not mistaken that its only purpose is for such, Karen Barer in Prayerideas.org lists some other examples while also including national healing:

"– Praying for those in a crisis situation who don't know God and/or who may not know how to pray or who don't believe in prayer.

– Praying for those who are living in opposition to God through their unhealthy lifestyle, pride or rebellion.

– Praying for communities, institutions, churches or workplaces where factions are battling for control.

– Praying against unjust circumstances, governments and laws.

– Praying for those who don't believe in God, or are angry at God or who are actively denouncing faith/religion

– Praying against cultural and social conditions that are corrupt, evil or destructive.

– Praying for the weak, ill, downtrodden or oppressed who cannot pray for themselves.

– Praying against evil and for the coming of God's Kingdom.

– Praying for those going through the stress of a major life crisis whose mental energy may be drained to the point where they are unable to pray for themselves." (Baber, 2013).

This may be the occasion in our national history to ask God to show us the way. He may need to tap us on the shoulder and show us what it is that we need to do now. We know that there is a gap developing in the wall of America. We may not know our role in standing in that gap to prevent further erosion. These are times when God whispers in our ear that it's time for us to move into action. God will show us where the gap that needs filling is. We then need to pray with authority. Authentic authority which we have as God's children made in His image.

The verse in Ezekiel reminds us that it only takes one person to intercede and worlds can change. Abraham and Moses were one, but they stood in the gap and changed history. Ezekiel, Abraham and Moses remind us that prayers are never insignificant. We must recognize what we are fighting. A longer version than before of Ephesians 6:12 goes on to explain: "for we are not fighting against flesh-and-blood enemies, but against evil rulers and authorities of the unseen world, against mighty powers in this dark world, and against evil spirits in the heavenly places."

If we were only fighting flesh and blood, we might be more invigorated to establish a defense and counter movement. However, the real enemy at work is beyond our grasp of a traditional struggle. That is why our only defense ultimately is prayer.

Moving Forward

The prophet Ezekiel provides these words from God that bear repeating. Ezekiel 22:30, "I looked for someone among them who would build up the wall and stand before me in the gap on behalf of the land, so I would not have to destroy it, but I found no one." (NIV). The King James version uses the word "hedge" instead of "wall". Where did He look? He looked to the prophets, but they had shied away from His Word. He looked to the priests, but they too had fallen away. He searched the whole of the population of Jerusalem. Ezekiel kept receiving the Word of God and gives a recount of the cost for falling away from the Word of God. God was looking for someone to intercede on behalf of the sinning Jerusalem. God was looking for that one person who could stand in the gap, so God could avoid passing judgement on Jerusalem. God sought to show mercy and love but needed that one soul to be the link between God and the people. God would later appoint a person to be the link between His world and Himself and that was Jesus. Jesus in essence stood in the gap for us. He provided the link between us and the greatness of God. Jesus's sacrifice should stand as an example for us when it comes to standing for the Gospel Truth. Our sacrifice in doing so will never be as great as His but we do need to stand up against the onslaught of bigotry and hate that continues to multiply openly. Without standing to prevent the anti-Christian movement, it will continue to advance without resistance. We need to take a stand and use the power within the laws and Constitution of this land to say, "enough is enough". Time has come to stop twisting the plain English of our laws and return to the absolute definitions and intent for which our laws were crafted. This country was founded on the Christian principles and it needs to return to those principles, or we'll find ourselves being Ezekiel's Jerusalem.

We are called to carry each other's burdens. Timothy explains one way how prayer is our most effective tool to stand in the gap and stop the advance of anti-Christianity. *"First of all, then, I urge that supplications, prayers, intercessions, and thanksgivings be made for all people ... This is good, and it is pleasing in the sight of God our Savior, who desires all people to be saved and to come to the knowledge of the truth."* 1 Timothy 2:1; 3-4. Prayer is an effective weapon against the perils of today. God likes prayer. We can use prayer to intercede for friends, neighbors, family and even the world. God can handle large and small issues, but He needs us to the intercessor on His behalf. We first need to realize that the message of misinformation is abundant and ongoing. Slowly but surely making headway into diverting the Christian way into their own politically correct, self-serving way. They use soft words and messages to hide the fact that there is a gap in the Christian wall, so we don't have to worry about repairing it or standing in it. Standing in the gap requires us to fight against the enemies of God to protect His people. The fight need not be passive. It must be persuasive. The church, the ministers and the congregants must continue to impress upon the need to continually be repenting of our sins. Our prayers should always acknowledge our need for God's mercy and His mercy on all people. We need our individual wall reinforced. For Satan to make headway in our home, in our lives, in the lives of those we love and with those we care, our wall must be at full strength. Scriptures remind us that if the individual wall is strong, it will not be breached. Our own wall is the first defense. If each Christian resolved to individually stand in the gap, then the anti-Christian onslaught will be stopped dead in its tracks. Let us not forget that the Holy Spirit is next to us at all times and will be within us if we open the door. With the help of the Holy Spirit our wall is impenetrable. We must be on guard against jealousy, backbiting, suspicion, and lies that even those close to us might thrust upon us. It is not only the barrage of anti-Christian sentiment that is at work in the larger world that we must fill the gap in defense but also the same can be happening to us in our smaller, inner world and there too, we need a defense. Fall back to prayer and open our hearts for the guidance of the Holy Spirit who is there to teach us, guide us and strengthen us. James 4:2 reminds us of the need to simply ask and if more were to ask the right questions about their discontent many things would start to right themselves Biblically. James stated: "You desire and do not have, so you murder. You covet and cannot obtain, so you fight and quarrel. You do not have, because you do not ask." How often the book of James impresses upon us to ask and ask with a heart of sincerity and it shall be given freely. Trust those words.

Non-Believing

Ultimately the war being waged is difficult if we cannot have an effective defense against the beliefs being held by those that do not want to hear the truth. Where is their authoritative truth? If there is not a standard by which a belief is based, it cannot be the same truth that another may hold. It is as simple as needing to have the same basis on which to base our judgement. Someone says it is nighttime and we agree because it is dark, and the moon is shining. Someone says it is daytime and we agree because the sun is shining. Somewhere, at the end of the line, there must be a standard by which we gauge our thoughts; an absolute standard that is the established authority.

Those not wishing to accept the authoritative Word of God seek to change the standard that is our reference. They do this by changing the definition of long establish words in the English vocabulary. We accept Scripture because we know that nothing can be taken from it and nothing can be added to it. The Scriptures are the Word of God. The principles in the Bible are the Christian standard on which Christians establish their moral beliefs. Others struggle and seek aimlessly to find fulfillment because they do not have the bedrock of the teachings in the Bible that provide purpose. We are made in God's image, we have value, we have a purpose on this earth, we have the Holy Spirit within us guiding us and we have the treasure of knowing that there is an eternal life and we know how to get it. Some deny the truth because it is personally painful for them to give in and accept their sin. Christians know they sin, and they know how to give that burden to Christ and move on. Some seek drugs and alternative lifestyles looking for happiness and fulfillment, but statistics will bear out that they are not finding it. Other beliefs are anti-Semitic and deny that Jesus is from the house of David and try to convince Christians that the Jewish people are the worst of world population. They bring in political policies trying to move the discussion away from their ultimate anti-Semitic objective. To all of this, they severely lack a gold standard that is the epidemy of the immovable backstop on which they base their beliefs. For Christians, the Word of God is that backstop. History has shown that the guiding principles of the Bible have guided mankind through centuries of tribulation and those following the Word are always vindicated in their faith to the Scriptures.

Family

The foundation of any society is the family unit. The best family unit is as how God designed it to be; husband, wife and children. Children's education begins and ends in the home. Their moral values are established by what they observe in the family. Their behavior is established from a young age by the dynamics and roles within the family unit.

Is it any wonder that we observe in society today so much hatred and bitter opinions when statistics continues to tell us that the traditional family unit is in a sharp decline? Children are raised with one struggling parent or really no caretaking parents and the schools work tirelessly to instill discipline in the classroom with no avail.

Is it possible for the unsavory hate and bitterness seen in front of us every night on the news be reversed by a simple move by America to restore the honor of the traditional family by some movement to celebrate the family design established by God? Cardinal Walter Kasper wen to so far as to write a whole book on the necessity of the family unit in a Christ oriented society. (Kasper, 2014).

After Cardinal Kasper's highlighting the role of the family, family focus did have its moment in the spotlight as noted from the Pope's promotion of family: "In his apostolic exhortation *The Joy of the Gospel*, Pope Francis wrote: *The family is experiencing a profound cultural crisis, as are all communities and social bonds. In the case of the family, the weakening of these bonds is particularly serious because the family is the fundamental cell of society, where we learn to live with others despite our differences and to belong to one another; it is also the place where parents pass on the faith to their children.*" (The Gospel of the Family, 2014).

One can find debate that the family unit is a Scripture advocated system. The following is a good rebuttal to those interpretations of selected Scripture. As has been a theme throughout this paper, selectively cited a piece of Scripture to fit your argument is a fraught fallacy. The below insertion covers both the misnomer that the church trumps the family system and provides excellent examples of Biblical reinforcement for the family whose advice could wholly change society if followed.

"Jesus did *not* say (for example, in Matthew 12:46-50 and Luke 14:26) that "the church trumps the family system." As a matter of fact, we think such an interpretation of His words can be dangerously misapplied. A great deal of damage has been inflicted on spouses and children through over-commitment to church programs and activities."

"What Jesus *did* say is that our love for *Him* should be so great and so overpowering that it eclipses all other loves. Even the strongest and most compelling of our natural human loves ought to look like "hate" when compared with our love for Christ. In other words, the depth of our commitment to Him is revealed precisely in our willingness to forsake even the very *best* things in life *if called upon to do so for His sake.*"

"And family *is* one of the very best and most important things in life. That's exactly what gives this "hard" saying of Jesus its peculiar force. The Bible makes this plain in the creation account, where God makes a woman and a man, unites them as "one flesh" and blesses them with the exhortation to "be fruitful and multiply" (Genesis 1:27, 28; 2:23, 24). It revisits the theme in Deuteronomy 11:19 and Proverbs 22:6, where the Lord instructs His people to train up their children in the way of holiness and truth. It underscores the message in the Psalmist's declaration that "children are a heritage from the Lord, the fruit of the womb is a reward" (Psalm 127:3). It emphasizes it in the apostle's solemn warning that "if anyone does not provide for his own, and especially for those of his household, he has denied the faith and is worse than an unbeliever" (1 Timothy 5:8). For all these reasons, we do not hesitate to affirm that there is a strong and inescapable biblical basis for "focusing on the family." (What the Bible Says About Family, 2019).

Equality Act, HR5

Now the anti-Christian movement gets serious with the reintroduction of a Democrat bill called the Equality Act. In proposing that LGBTQ be added to the 1964 Civil Rights Act specifying protected classes, it also proposes that the Religious Freedom Restoration Act cannot be used in civil rights arguments. In other words, religious beliefs cannot be used as a reason to discriminate. At least two Supreme Court cases are on the issue of religious beliefs and the application of artistic talents being forced to do a service against their closely held religious beliefs. The Colorado case was a win for religious beliefs but only marginally and within very narrow parameters. The Equality Act would make sure that such cases in the future would be won by the LGBTQ community by outlawing one's right to refuse service if the service would require them to do something against their religious belief.

In Congress, the Equality Act is now in the hearing and markup stage which makes it closer to being voted on by the floor. There are additions to protected classes and the bill names age, disability, gender reassignment, race, religion or belief, sex, sexual orientation, marriage and civil partnership and pregnancy and maternity. The additions are gender reassignment, sexual orientation, civil partnership and pregnancy and maternity. The later of course would nullify certain abortion restriction laws in a number of conservative states. The fine print essentially nullifies any restriction to a woman's right to do as she chooses with her body and biology.

As with many exercises of giving protected status, someone else is losing status. Two groups would be losers of position. Blacks and women (women who are not LGBTQ) would lose their premier status given in the current non-discrimination law. Other losers would be employers and workers, medical professionals, parents and children, and non-profits and volunteers. The ramifications of the Equality Act for each of the above-mentioned groups is very much an attack on the family and parenting to the extent that personal teaching at home and in the school would be regulated by the government and outcast parents of virtually any influence over their children. One family lost their daughter to the court in Ohio because they would not support a testosterone treatment for her. These types of pulling children from their parents over disagreements on sex change inclinations would be prolific under the Equality Act. Doctors and medical professionals would not be able to exercise certain therapies even when their best medical judgement says otherwise.

The open bathroom debate is ongoing with some retailers such as Target allowing patrons to use whatever restroom or changing room they wish. The stronger argument here should be immediately obvious. It is an invitation for perverse activity that does not require much imagination to visualize. Predators will take advantage of such leeway.

Women lose tremendously, and all non-LGBTQ women should be in open revolt of the Act. It would eliminate the entire women's sports idea because now males identifying as female can compete in their sports. Women lose their privacy in public and no public restroom or change room is necessarily a safe place for a woman to be. Mothers would lose influence over the guidance of their children.

As is always the case, giving rights to one group almost always means restricting rights to another. The Equality Act leans so heavily towards protecting the LGBTQ community that the majority of Americans would have to surrender rights. The small insert regarding the Religious Freedom Restoration Act would in reality shut down one's right to their religious beliefs virtually making many Christian doctrines illegal. Some say this Act would even work its way inside the church where pastors are restricted from preaching certain doctrines even within the walls of the church.

Some say that the Equality Act (HR5) would put a class of men above women suggesting that a transgender male has greater protection than a biological female in virtually every venue. The worst of the Bill is its placement of attitude and mannerisms out rank biology as a science by which gender is defined. Regardless of how hard this notion is pushed, in the end the chromosomes don't change. You are either XX or XY and changing how you dress or what kind of medical procedure you go through; the chromosomes remain true to their creation identity.

The Act attempts to use legislation to coerce those people who do not accept LGBTQ ideologies to fall in line despite their disapproval. It is as if the Democrats belief that they can control and change the values and beliefs held by millions of Americans by legislation and force. They have for the past decade failed to move Americans towards liberalization by other means so now they are pushing to use the powers of government to change the heartland values. This has never worked in the history of mankind and will lead to ultimate massive dishevel in American society.

The religious belief implications are enormous. A well-earned degree of support was given religion under the Religious Freedom Restoration Act and that support is completely nullified by HR5. It is, as some say, another attempt to criminalize Christian religious beliefs. Particularly the belief about marriage between a man and a woman and that homosexuality is a sin. It also works against the first Amendment of the Constitution regarding religious freedom. The framers of the Constitution intentionally did not restrict what the beliefs of a religion are but HR5 would essentially define what you can belief in public and what you cannot.

Will the Equality Act make it into law? Not likely. It will undoubtedly pass the House of Representatives now controlled by the Democrats but die in the Republican held Senate. The other backstop of course is a veto at the Executive level which requires a two-thirds majority vote to overturn. This presently is a pretty high bar to cross. The warning is out. Democrats and their LGBTQ supporters are making inroads and every year they inch closer to moving within our own homes to force acceptance of their behavior. This is a time to stand in gap and get serious about intercessory prayer because these are our last and strongest means of restoring America to its Christian roots. Franklin Graham recently stood in the gap regarding Gay Democrat and presidential candidate Pete Buttigieg. Graham delivered the truth and suffered innumerable personal attacks for speaking what Christians know to simply be the truth.

Stand in the gap, pray the intercessory prayers and never give up your God given rights. Don't pick Scriptures without exploring their context and investigating their theological interpretations. Open your heart to the Holy Spirit and appreciate the power that is yours. Do not be timid about what you believe and accept that at times we must be very public about our Christian stance.

BIBLIOGRAPHY

(2019). Retrieved from America Right to Life: https://www.youtube.com/watch?v=WBQInTgB-7s

5 Evidences the Bible is True. (2019). Retrieved from Focus on the Family: https://www.bringyourbible.org/5-evidences-the-bible-is-true/

Adamson, D. (2019, April 12). *Dave Adamson: The Price of Christian Free Speech*. Retrieved from Fox News: https://www.foxnews.com/opinion/christian-free-speech

American Patriotism and Christian Worship. (2016, June 30). Retrieved from The Witness: https://thewitnessbcc.com/american-patriotism-and-christian-worship/

Americans Divided on the Importance of Church. (2014, March 24). Retrieved from Barna: https://www.barna.com/research/americans-divided-on-the-importance-of-church/#.UzwMlq1dW7o

Appell, L. D. (2019, January 31). *Virginia is for infanticide? Abortion bill leaves me shocked by what's going on in my own state*. Retrieved from Fox News: https://www.foxnews.com/opinion/virginia-is-for-infanticide-abortion-bill-leaves-me-shocked-by-whats-going-on-in-my-own-state

Baber, K. (2013, June 26). *How to Stand in the Gap in Prayer*. Retrieved from Prayer Ideas: https://prayerideas.org/how_to_pray/intercession/how-to-stand-in-the-gap-in-prayer/

Baldwin, R. (2017, June 30). *3 Characteristics of Biblical Authenticity*. Retrieved from Authentic Manhood: https://www.authenticmanhood. com/3-characteristics-of-biblical-authenticity/

Ball, L. (2018, March 18). *Open Borders and the Bible*. Retrieved from The Aquila Report: https://www.theaquilareport.com/ open-borders-and-the-bible/

Barber, D. (2018, January 09). *The Effects of Revolution & Rotation on Climate & Weather*. Retrieved from Sciencing: https://sciencing.com/ about-6737591-effect-revolution-rotation-climate-weather.html

Barnhart, M. (2019, February 21). *Amanda Palmer's baby "abortion shower' song actually makes a pro-life argument, critic says*. Retrieved from Christian Post: https://www.christianpost.com/news/amanda-palmer-abortion-baby-shower-song-pro-life-message.html

Beinart, P. (2017, April). *Breaking Faith*. Retrieved from The Atlantic: https://www.theatlantic.com/magazine/archive/2017/04/ breaking-faith/517785/

Bentley, C. (2019, February 15). *What does the Bible say about the Green New Deal?* Retrieved from The Christian Post: https://www.christianpost. com/voice/bible-green-new-deal.html

Berke, J. (2018, August 07). *One of the largest banks issued an alarming warning that Earth is running out of the resources to sustain life*. Retrieved from Business Insider: https://www.businessinsider.com/ hsbc-warns-earth-is-running-out-of-resources-for-life-2018-8

Berry, D. S. (2019, February 22). *The Trump Adminstration issued a final rule Friday that underscores that federal taxpayer funds ...* Retrieved from Breitbart: https://www.breitbart.com/education/2019/02/22/ donald-trump-administration-abortion-is-not-family-planning/

Blair, L. (2019, March 19). *Elizabeth Warren says words of Jesus, judgement of 'sheep and goats,' is driving force in her life*. Retrieved from Christian

Post: https://www.christianpost.com/news/elizabeth-warren-says-words-of-jesus-judgement-of-sheep-and-goats-is-driving-force-in-her-life.html

Blake, A. (2017, September 07). *Did Dianne Feinstein accuse a judicial nominee of being too Christian?* Retrieved from Washington Post: https://www.washingtonpost.com/news/the-fix/wp/2017/09/07/did-a-democratic-senator-just-accuse-a-judicial-nominee-of-being-too-christian/?noredirect=on&utm_term=.6ffbd7d22d8b

Bloom, J. (2015, May 18). *Christian, Your Job Is a Ministry Job.* Retrieved from desiringGod.org: https://www.desiringgod.org/articles/christian-your-job-is-a-ministry-job

Bois, P. (2019, February 22). *Couple Sues Planned Parenthood for Child Support afte Failed Abortion.* Retrieved from Daily Wire: https://www.dailywire.com/news/43837/couple-sues-planned-parenthood-child-support-after-paul-bois

Bolton, B. (2019). *God is So Not Pro-Life.* Retrieved from Freedom from Religion Foundation: https://ffrf.org/component/k2/item/25602-abortion-rights

Bradley, M. (2018, December 27). *Pride Cometh Before the Fall.* Retrieved from Bibleknowledge.com.

Brown, C. (2016, October 14). *The Two Ways God Wants You to Use Your Talents.* Retrieved from Stewardship: https://www.stewardship.com/articles/the-two-ways-god-wants-you-to-use-your-talents

Butters, J. (2019). *Why America Can't Separate Religion & Politics.* Retrieved from BU College of Arts & Sciences: http://www.bu.edu/cas/magazine/fall15/america/

Byard, E. (2019, January 17). *Karen Pence Should Not Be Teaching at an Anti-LGBTQ School.* Retrieved from

The Daily Beast: https://www.thedailybeast.com/karen-pence-should-not-be-teaching-at-an-anti-lgbtq-school

Cadwaladr, E. (2018, April 01). *The Anti-Christian Movement*. Retrieved from American Thinker: https://www.americanthinker.com/articles/2018/04/the_antichristian_movement.html

Callaway, C. (2019). *Religion & Politics*. Retrieved from Internet Encyclopedia of Philosophy: https://www.iep.utm.edu/rel-poli/

Campbell, B. J. (2018, October 30). *Social Justice is a Crowdsourced Religion*. Retrieved from Handwaving Freakoutery: https://medium.com/handwaving-freakoutery/social-justice-is-a-crowdsourced-religion-87dc3ae3a82b

Caplan, J. (2019, April 20). *April Ryan Freaks on Mike Huckabee: 'Will You Get into Heaven? The Answer is No!'*. Retrieved from Breitbart: https://www.breitbart.com/politics/2019/04/20/april-ryan-freaks-on-mike-huckabee-will-you-get-into-heaven-the-answer-is-no/

Carson, D. (2010, October 18). *TGC Asks Don Carson: How Do We Work for Justice and Not Undermine Evangelism?* Retrieved from TGC: https://www.thegospelcoalition.org/article/asks-carson-justice-evangelism/

Carter, J. (2015, March 17). *FactChecker: Are All Christian Denominations in Decline?* . Retrieved from The Gospel Coalition: https://www.thegospelcoalition.org/article/factchecker-are-all-christian-denominations-in-decline/

Carter, J. (2018, August 17). *The FAQs: What Chriatians Should Know About Social Justice*. Retrieved from The Gospel Coalition: https;//www.thegospelcoalition.org/article/faqs-christians-know-social-justice/

Choosing a New Church or House of Worship. (2016, August 23). Retrieved from Pew Research: http://www.pewforum.org/2016/08/23/1-the-search-for-a-new-congregation/

Christianity, A. (2019, February 19). *What is the Christian view on abortion?* Retrieved from Active Christianity: https://activechristianity.org/abortion-a-christian-perspective

Cole, S. J. (2005). *Lesson 17: The Sin of Judging Others (James 4:11-12)*. Retrieved from Bible.org: https://bible.org/seriespage/lesson-17-sin-judging-others-james-411-12

Cole, S. J. (2015, November 08). *Lesson 2: Authentic Christianity (Colossians 1:3-8)*. Retrieved from Bible.org: https://bible.org/seriespage/lesson-2-authentic-christianity-colossians-13-8

Copeland, L. (2019, January 17). *What God's Word Says About Abortion*. Retrieved from Living Waters: https://www.livingwaters.com/gods-word-says-abortion/

Corporate. (2017). *What Does the Bible Say About Abortion?* Retrieved from American Right to Life: http://americanrtl.org/what-does-the-bible-say-about-abortion

Crow, J. (2017, October 19). *7 Symptoms of a Prideful Heart*. Retrieved from Crosswalk: http://www.crosswalk.com/faith/spiritual-life/7-symptoms-of-a-prideful-heart.htm./

D McMinn, S. J. (2017, December). *Does pride really come before a fall? Longitudinal analysis of older English adults*. Retrieved from The BMJ: https://www.bmj.com/content/359/bmj.j5451

Dallas, K. (2018, October 29). *Why the relationship between religion and politics is more complicated than you think*. Retrieved from The Deseret News: https://www.deseretnews.com/article/900039417/why-the-relationship-between-religion-and-politics-is-more-complicated-than-you-think.html

Daniel Cox, R. P. (2017, September 06). *Public Religion Research Institute*. Retrieved from America's Changing

Religious Identity: https://www.prri.org/research/american-religious-landscape-christian-religiously-unaffiliated/

Data. (n.d.). Retrieved February 10, 2019, from GlobalChange.gov: https://www.globalchange.gov/browse/datasets

Davis, L. C. (2016, February 05). *Do Emotions and Morality Mix?* Retrieved from Science: https://www.theatlantic.com/science/archive/2016/02/how-do-emotions-sway-moral-thinking/460014/

Davis, W. (2019, January 16). *Liberal Groups Bash Karen Pence For Teaching At Christian School.* Retrieved from The Daily Caller: https://dailycaller.com/2019/01/16/liberal-groups-bash-karen-pence-christian-school/

Dempsey, J. (2018, February 08). *Media Disdain for Christians.* Retrieved from Liberty Nation: https://www.libertynation.com/media-disdain-for-christians/

Denison, J. (2019, March 18). *The college scam, Felicity Huffman, and Lori Loughlin: Two Biblical Responses.* Retrieved from Christian Post: https://www.christianpost.com/voice/the-college-scam-felicity-huffman-and-lori-loughlin-two-biblical-responses.html

Dennis Englin, J. F. (2017, September 11). *Climate Change.* Retrieved from The Master's University: https://www.masters.edu/news/climatechange.html

DeSanctis, A. (2017, September 06). *Dianne Feinstein Attacks Judicial Nominee's Catholic Faith* . Retrieved from National Review: https://www.nationalreview.com/corner/dianne-feinstein-amy-coney-barrett-senator-attacks-catholic-judicial-nominee/

Donovan, R. N. (2009). *Matthew 25:31-46 Biblical Commentary:.* Retrieved from Sermon Writer: https://www.sermonwriter.com/biblical-commentary/matthew-2531-46/

Douglas, P. (2017, April 22). *Christian Earth Day lessons: worship by protecting creation* . Retrieved from The Gaurdian: https://www.theguardian.com/environment/climate-consensus-97-per-cent/2017/apr/22/christian-earth-day-lessons-worship-by-protectiong-creation

Drollinger, R. (2019, March 19). *What the Bible Says About Our Illegal Immigration Problem*. Retrieved from Capitol Ministries: https://capmin.org/author/r-and-d/

Dunnett, W. M. (2019). *Pride.* Retrieved from Bible Study Tools: https://www.biblestudytools.com/dictionary/pride/

Edwards, L. (2010, May 10). *Psychologists say babies know right from wrong even at six months*. Retrieved from Medical Xpress: https://medicalxpress.com/news/2010-05-psychologists-babies-wrong-months.html

Ellis, C. (2019, April 16). *Churches Desecrated in Ongoing Attacks Across Europe*. Retrieved from CBN News: https://www1.cbn.com/cbnnews/us/2019/april/churches-desecrated-in-ongoing-attacks-across-europe

Erickson, C. (2018, June 04). *Biblical Justice & Social Justice*. Retrieved from Just Faith Summit: http://www.sharedhope.org/2018/06/biblical-justice-and-social-justice/

Exodus 21. (2019). Retrieved from Biblia.com: https://biblia.com/bible/Exodus21.1-36

Fairchild, M. (2018, September 24). *How Many Christians Are In the World Today?* . Retrieved from ThoughtCo: https://www.thoughtco.com/christianity-statistics-700533

Faith on the Hill. (2019, January 03). Retrieved from Pew Research: http://www.pewforum.org/topics/religion-and-politics

Fischer, B. (2014, July 09). *The Bible and borders*. Retrieved from Renew America: https://www.renewamerica.com/columns/fischer/140709

Fischer, B. (2019, January 23). *Russell Moore Mangles Matthew 25*. Retrieved from American Family Association: https://www.afa.net/the-stand/faith/2019/01/russell-moore-mangles-matthew-25/

Foust, M. (2019, January 21). *Lady Gaga Says Mike Pence Is 'Worst Representation' of Christianity*. Retrieved from The Christian Headlines: https://www.christianheadlines.com/contributors/michael-foust/lady-gaga-says-mike-pence-is-worst-representation-of-christianity.html

Foust, M. (2019, January 21). *Lady Gaga Says Mike Pence Is 'Worst Representation' of Christianity*. Retrieved from Christian Headlines: https://www.christianheadlines.com/contributors/michael-foust/lady-gaga-says-mike-pence-is-worst-representation-of-christianity.html

French, D. (2019, January 17). *Karen Pence, Are You Now, or Have You Ever Been, Part of a Christian Ministry?* Retrieved from The National Review: https://www.nationalreview.com/2019/01/karen-pence-are-you-now-or-have-you-ever-been-part-of-a-christian-ministry/

Gewertz, K. (2007, May 03). *Is doing the right thing hard-wired?* Retrieved from The Harvard Gazzette: https://news.harvard.edu/gazette/story/2007/05/is-doing-the-right-thing-hard-wired/

Gill, J. (2019, January 29). *Democrats To Remove God, Gender-Specific Language From Committee Oath*. Retrieved from Daily Caller: https://dailycaller.com/2019/01/29/democrats-remove-god-oath/

Gliddon, L. S. (2002). *Purpose of Angels*. Retrieved from All About God: https://www.allaboutgod.com/purpose-of-angels-faq.htm

Graham, F. (2019, January 30). *Billy Graham Evangelical Association*. Retrieved from Billy Graham Evangelical Association: https://billygraham.org/decision-magazine/february-2019/when-truth-is-labeled-hate-speech/

Granberg-Michael, W. (2019, January 11). *Where Is Christianity Headed? The View from 2019*. Retrieved from Christian Headlines: https://

www.christianheadlines.com/columnists/guest-commentary/where-is-christianity-headed-the-view-from-2019.html

Grudem, W. (2018, July 02). *Why Building a Border Wall Is a Morally Good Action*. Retrieved from Townhall: https://townhall.com/columnists/waynegrudem/2018/07/02/why-building-a-border-wall-is-a-morally-good-action-n2496574

Gruden, W. (1994). *Sytematic Theoloty*. Grand Rapids: Zondervan.

Gryboski, M. (2019, February 22). *Trump admin. finalizes federal rule barring funding of abortion through Title X*. Retrieved from Christian Post: https://www.christianpost.com/news/trump-admin-finalizes-federal-rule-barring-funding-of-abortion-through-title-x.html

Guzik, D. (2018). *Matthew 25 – Jesus' Olivet Discourse (Part 2)*. Retrieved from Enduring Word: https://enduringword.com/bible-commentary/matthew-25/

Haag, M. (2019, January 16). *Karen Pence Is Teaching at Christian School That Bars L.G.B.T. Students and Teachers*. Retrieved from New York Times: https://www.nytimes.com/2019/01/16/us/politics/karen-pence-school-lgbt-ban.html

Haag, M. (2019, January 16). *Karen Pence Is Teaching at Christian School That Bars L.G.B.T. Students and Teachers*. Retrieved from New York Times: https://www.nytimes.com/2019/01/16/us/politics/karen-pence-school-lgbt-ban.html

Hagin, K. E. (2019). *Authority in the Name of Jesus*. Retrieved from Hope.Faith.Prayer: https://www.hopefaithprayer.com/authority-name-jesus-hagin/

Hall, E. (2019, January 16). *Karen Pence Is Teaching At A Christian School That Bans LGBT Students And Employees*. Retrieved from BuzzFeed News: https://www.buzzfeednews.com/article/ellievhall/karen-pence-teaching-christian-school-bans-lgbt

Hamill, J. (2018, April 16). *What Does The Bible Say About Abortion?* Retrieved from Atheist Ireland: https://atheist.ie/2018/04/what-does-the-bible-say-about-abortion/

Hoeven, E. (2019, January 31). *The new frontlines in the battle over late-term abortions: Why a new law in New York and one proposed in Virginia alarm the pro-life movement.* Retrieved from Deseret News: https://www.deseretnews.com/article/900053358/the-new-frontlines-in-the-battle-over-late-term-trimester-abortions-why-a-new-law-in-new-york-and-one-proposed-in-virginia-alarm-the-pro-life-movement-reproductive-health-act-2019.html

Holmes, J. (2018, September 06). *What Does 'Social Justice" Really Mean.* Retrieved from Relevant Magazine: https://www.relevantmagazine.com/current/what-soes-social-justice-really-mean/

Ingber, S. (2019, January 29). *Pakistan's Supreme Court Upholds Christian Woman's Blasphemy Acquittal.* Retrieved from NPR: https://www.npr.org/2019/01/29/689611827/pakistans-supreme-court-upholds-christian-woman-s-blasphemy-acquittal

Is there power in the name of Jesus? (2019, February 14). Retrieved from Got Questions: https://www.gotquestions.org/power-in-the-name-of-Jesus.html

Jamieson, B. (2019). *A Deeper Look at What the Bible Says about Truth.* Retrieved from Explore God: https://www.exploregod.com/what-the-bible-says-about-truth-paper

John R. Edwards, J. (2009, September 16). *A Biblical Perspective on Immigration Policy.* Retrieved from Center for Immigration Studies: https://cis.org/Report/Biblical-Perspective-Immigration-Policy/

John Stonestreet, G. S. (2019, February 12). *The Green New Deal: Government Is Not Our Savior.* Retrieved from Christian Headlines: https://www.christianheadlines.com/columnists/breakpoint/the-green-new-deal-government-is-not-our-savior.html

Johnson, M. Z. (2016, January 17). *Don't Believe in Christian Privilege? These 15 Examples Will Leave No Doubt.* Retrieved from Everyday Feminism: https://everydayfeminism.com/2016/01/believing-christian-privilege/

Jones, E. (2015, January). *Modern Christianity has evolved throughout the centuries and continues to adapt today. But did Jusus intend the religion He founded to evolve?* Retrieved from Life, Hope & Truth: https://lifehopeandtruth.com/change/the-church/was-christianity-designed-to-evolve/

Kasper, C. W. (2014). *The Gospel of the Family.* Retrieved from Paullist Press: https://www.paulistpress.com/Products/8-452-4/the-gospel-of-the-family.aspx

Kennebrew, D. A. (2012, November 06). *What is true worship?* Retrieved from Christian Bible Studies: https://www.christianitytoday.com/biblestudies/bible-answers/spirituallife/what-is-true-worship.html

Killermann, S. (2012, May 14). *30+ Examples of Christian Privilege.* Retrieved from It's Pronounced Metrosexual: https://www.itspronouncedmetrosexual.com/2012/05/list-of-examples-of-christian-privileg/

Klett, L. M. (2019, January 29). *JD Greear: 'White privilege' exists; here's what Christians can do.* Retrieved from The Christian Post: https://www.christianpost.com/news/jd-greear-white-privilege-exists-heres-what-christians-can-do.html

Klusendorf, S. (2019). *DEAD SILENCE: MUST THE BIBLE SAY ABORTION IS WRONG BEFORE WE CAN KNOW IT'S WRONG?* Retrieved from One Place: https://www.oneplace.com/ministries/bible-answer-man/read/articles/dead-silence-must-the-bible-say-abortion-is-wrong-before-we-can-know-its-wrong-by-scott-klusendorf-16687.html

Kruger, M. J. (2018, April 09). *New Series: The 10 Commandments of Progressive Christianity.* Retrieved from Canon Fodder: https://www.michaeljkruger.com/new-series-the-10-commandments-of-progressive-christianity/

Leo XIII. (n.d.). Rerum Novarum,. n. 26.

Limbaugh, D. (2018, July 11). *Limbaugh: The Democratic Party's Christian problem*. Retrieved from The Spectrum: https://www.thespectrum.com/story/opinion/2018/07/11/liberal-left-waging-war-against-christian-ideals/775740002/

Limbaugh, D. (2019, March 22). *Liberalism Is Dehumanizing*. Retrieved from Townhall: https://townhall.com/columnists/davidlimbaugh/2019/03/22/liberalism-is-dehumanizing-n2543522

Livingstone, M. (2016, March 17). *5 Reasons the church must teach the Bible*. Retrieved from Mike Livingstone: https://mikelivingstone.com/2016/03/17/5-reasons-the-church-priortize-bible-teaching/

Louis Casiano, S. S. (2019, April 21). *Easter Sunday explosions at multiple churches and hotels rock Sri Lanka, death toll rises past 200*. Retrieved from Fox News: https://www.foxnews.com/world/easter-sunday-explosions-at-multiple-churches-and-hotels-rock-sri-lanka-death-tolls-rises

MacFarland, A. (2019). *Defending the Faith*. Retrieved from Focus on the Family: https://www.focusonthefamily.com/faith/faith-in-life/defending-the-faith/take-a-stand

Maren, J. v. (2017, November 10). *Progressives have long disdained Christians, but now they're declaring open war* . Retrieved from Life Site:https://www.lifesitenews.com/opinion/progressives-have-long-disdained-christians-but-now-theyre-declaring-open-w

Markl, D. (2011, October 14). *Social Justice in the Bible*. Retrieved from Thinking Faith: https://www.thinkingfaith.org/articles/20111014_1.htm

Martin, J. (2009). *Evangelizing Environmentalism: A Vision for a*. Toledo: University of Toledo.

Massaro, T. W. (2017, August 27). *4 Reasons You Should Care about Secularism*. Retrieved from Core Christianity: https://corechristianity.com/resource-library/articles/4-reasons-you-should-care-about-secularization

Mattson, S. (2015, February 11). *Social Justice Is a Christian Tradition — Not a Liberal Agenda*. Retrieved from Sojourners: https://sojo.net/articles/social-justice-christian-tradition-not-liberal-agenda

May, T. (2018, December 17). *Would Human Extinction Be a Tragedy?* Retrieved from The New York Times: https://www.nytimes.com/2018/12/17/opinion/human-extinction-climate-change.html

McFarland, A. (2019, January 16). *Our Abandonment of Moral Law Is the Loss No One Is Talking About*. Retrieved from Alex McFarland: https://alexmcfarland.com/media/alex-mcfarland-our-abandonment-of-moral-law-is-the-loss-no-one-is-talking-about/

McFarland, D. A. (2019, January 16). *Alex McFarland: Our Abandonment of Moral Law Is the Loss No One Is Talking About*. Retrieved from Alex McFarland: https://alexmcfarland.com/media/alex-mcfarland-our-abandonment-of-moral-law-is-the-loss-no-one-is-talking-about/

Miller, E. C. (2018, November 13). *What Is the Future of the Evangelical-Republican Coalition?* Retrieved from Religion & Politics: https://religionandpolitics.org/2018/11/13/what-is-the-future-of-the-evangelical-republican-coalition/

Moons, M. (2019, February 04). *Phil Robertson: America Has to Be Godly Again to Be Great Again*. Retrieved from Breitbart News: https://www.breitbart.com/politics/2019/02/04/phil-robertsons-america-has-to-be-godly-again-to-be-great-again/

Moral Reasoning. (2018, August 27). Retrieved from Stanford Encyclopedia of Philosophy: https://plato.stanford.edu/entries/reasoning-moral/

Morrison, M. (2019, January 24). *Inspiration, Authority, and Reliability of the Bible, by Michael Morrison.* Retrieved from Grace Communion Seminary: https://www.gcs.edu/mod/page/view.php?id=4246

Morse, B. (2019, April 22). *Sri Lanka Attack Suspect: "Anyone Who Disagrees With Muslims Should be Killed".* Retrieved from Red State: https://www.redstate.com/brandon_morse/2019/04/22/sri-lanka-attack-suspect-%e2%80%9canyone-disagrees-muslims-killed%e2%80%9d/

Muehlenberg, B. (2019, March 19). *Defending Faith in an Anti-Faith Age.* Retrieved from CultureWatch: https://billmuehlenberg.com/2019/02/25/defending-faith-in-an-anti-faith-age/

North, A. (2019, February 01). *The controversy around Virginia's new abortion bill, explained.* Retrieved from Vox: https://www.vox.com/2019/2/1/18205428/virginia-abortion-bill-kathy-tran-ralph-northam

Novak, M. (2009, December 29). *Social Justice: Not What You Think It Is.* Retrieved from The Heritage Foundation: https://www.heritage.org/poverty-and-inequality/report/social-justice-not-what-you-think-it

O'Kane, C. (2019, January 24). *New York passes law allowing abortions at any time if mother's health is at risk.* Retrieved from CBS: https://www.cbsnews.com/news/new-york-passes-abortion-bill-late-term-if-mothers-health-is-at-risk-today-2019-01-23/

O'Neil, T. (2017, January 24). *Pelosi: Democrats Do 'the Lord's Work,' Republicans 'Dishonor God'.* Retrieved from P J Media: https://pjmedia.com/faith/2017/01/24/pelosi-democrats-do-the-lords-work-republicans-dishonor-god/

Oppel, W. (2007). *The Mosaic Generation: The future of Christianity? Who are they and how will they change the future?* Retrieved from Leadership Advance Online: https://www.regent.edu/acad/global/publications/lao/issur_7/oppel.htm

O'Reilly, A. (2017, December 24). *Dems challenge Trump judicial nominee over Knights of Columbus membership*. Retrieved from Fox News: https://www.foxnews.com/politics/harris-and-hirono-question-federal-judicial-nominee-over-knights-of-columbus-membership

O'Reilly, A. (2018, December 24). *Dems challenge Trump judicial nominee over Knights of Columbus membership*. Retrieved from Fox News: https://www.foxnews.com/politics/harris-and-hirono-question-federal-judicial-nominee-over-knights-of-columbus-membership

O'Reilly, A. (2018, December 24). *Dems challenge Trump judicial nominee over Knights of Columbus membership*. Retrieved from Fox News: https://www.foxnews.com/politics/harris-and-hirono-question-federal-judicial-nominee-over-knights-of-columbus-membership

Parker, A. (2019, January 31). *Clueless Loyola Prof. Declares War on Ben Shapiro Appearance: He's 'Linked to Numerous Hate Groups'*. Retrieved from Red State: https://www.redstate.com/alexparker/2019/01/31/nina-lozano-loyola-marymount-ben-shapiro-hate-speech-hate-groups/

Passi-Klaus, S. (2015, April 17). *Christians and Creation: 'You can't love God and ignore the Earth'*. Retrieved from The People of the United Methodist Church: http://www.umc.org/what-we-believe/christians-and-earth-day-you-cant-love-god-and-ignore-earth

Perkins, T. (2019, January 30). *Nancy Pelosi's God Problem*. Retrieved from Washington Update: https://www.frc.org/updatearticle/20190130/pelosi-problem

Perry, D. (2019, January 20). *Christian Schools Like Karen Pence's Are The Real Threat To Academic Freedom*. Retrieved from The Huffington Post: https://www.huffingtonpost.com/entry/opinion-karen-pence-christian-school_us_5c433eebe4b0a8dbe171d3f3

Pilote, A. (2014, January 01). *To render to each his due* . Retrieved from Michael: https://www.michaeljournal.org/articles/editorial/item/to-render-to-each-his-due

Poff, J. (2019, January 19). *FAKE NEWS! CNN Claims 'Around 1000' People Attended March for Life*. Retrieved from Todd Starnes: https://www.toddstarnes.com/faith/fake-news-cnn-claims-around-1000-people-attended-march-for-life/

Politics in the Bible. (2019). Retrieved from Christians in Politics: http://www.christiansinpolitics.org.uk/politics-in-the-bible/

Pollak, J. B. (2019, April 22). *Obama, Clinton, Democrats Denounce Attacks on 'Easter Worshippers,' Not 'Christians'*. Retrieved from Breitbart: https://www.breitbart.com/national-security/2019/04/22/obama-clinton-democrats-denounce-attacks-on-easter-worshippers-not-christians/

Prevo, J. (2019, January 30). *Why Do Many Pastors Avoid Warning Against Homosexuality and Abortion?* Retrieved from Billy Graham Evangelistic Association: https://billygraham.org/decision-magazine/february-2019/silent-about-sin-why-do-many-pastors-avoid-warning-against-homosexuality-and-abortion/

Przybylski, D. (2015, June 10). *Praying in the Powerful Name of Jesus*. Retrieved from Crosswalk: https://www.crosswalk.com/faith/prayer/praying-in-the-powerful-name-of-jesus.html

Quinn, L. (2019, March 19). *MSNBC host Joe Scarborough says Trump is 'antithesis' of Bible's teachings in wake of Evangelical survey*. Retrieved from Fox News: https://www.foxnews.com/entertainment/msnbc-host-joe-scarborough-says-trump-is-antithesis-of-bibles-teachings-after-evangelical-survey

Rasmussen, S. (2019, January 31). *What the Covington High School Incident Tells Us About America*. Retrieved from Townhall: https://townhall.com/columnists/scottrasmussen/2019/01/31/what-the-covington-high-school-incident-tells-us-about-america-n2540550

Rasmussen, S. (2019, January 31). *What the Covington High School Incident Tells Us About America*. Retrieved from Townhall: https://townhall.

com/columnists/scottrasmussen/2019/01/31/what-the-covington-high-school-incident-tells-us-about-america-n2540550

Religious Statements on Climate Change. (2019). Retrieved from Interfaith Power & Light: https://www.interfaithpowerandlight.org/religious-statements-on-climate-change/

Rivera, J. S. (2019, January 31). *BreakPoint: Do Religious Fundamentalist Have Brain Damage? The "Just-So Stories" Masquerading as Science.* Retrieved from BreakPoint: http://www.breakpoint.org/2019/01/breakpoint-do-religious-fundamentalist-have-brain-damage/

Rivera, J. S. (2019, January 31). *BreakPoint: Do Religious Fundamentalists Have Brain Damage?* Retrieved from Breakpoint.org: http://www.breakpoint.org/2019/01/breakpoint-do-religious-fundamentalist-have-brain-damage/

Robert P. Jones, D. C. (2016, October 19). *Clinton Maintains Double-digit Lead over Trump.* Retrieved from PRRI: http://www.prri.org/research/prri-brookings-oct-19-poll-politics-election-clinton-double-digit-lead-trump/

Rocklin, D. (2011, May). *DUELING DUALISMS: CHRISTIAN.* St. Paul: MACALESTER COLLEGE.

Roe v. Wade. (2019, February 19). Retrieved from Wikipedia: https://en.wikipedia.org/wiki/Roe_v._Wade

Sacks, E. (2018, April 22). *The gospel of climate change: Green pastors bringing environmentalism to evangelicals.* Retrieved from NEWS: https://www.nbcnews.com/news/religion/climate-change-schism-evangelical-christians-divided-human-role-global-warming-n865081

Sacks, E. (2018, April 23). *The gospel of climate change: Green pastors bringing environmentalism to evangelicals.* Retrieved from https://www.nbcnews.com/news/religion/climate-change-schism-evangelical-christians-divided-human-role-global-warming-n865081

Sandstrom, A. (2017, January 03). *Faith on the Hill*. Retrieved from Pew Research: http://www.pewforum.org/topics/religion-and-politics

Schoonover, R. Z. (2008). Defending Christianity in a Secular Culture. *Enrichment Journal*(Fall). Retrieved from RZIM: https://www.rzim.org/read/just-thinking-magazine/defending-christianity-in-a-secular-culture

Schulman, B. J. (2019). *Bruce J. Schulman*. Retrieved from Boston College Faculty: http://www.bu.edu/history/faculty/bruce-j-schulman/

Shapiro, A. (2019, January 31). *Failed Virginia Bill Sparks National Debate About Abortion*. Retrieved from NPR: https://www.npr.org/2019/01/31/690468965/failed-virginia-bill-sparks-national-debate-about-abortion

Shelton, J. S. (2019, February 28). *Theology and Border Walls*. Retrieved from Providence: https://providencemag.com/2019/02/christian-theology-border-walls/

Showalter, B. (2019, March 19). *Christian journalist to be interrogated by police for 'misgendering' activist's transgender child*. Retrieved from Christian Post: https://www.christianpost.com/news/christian-journalist-to-be-interrogated-by-police-for-misgendering-activists-transgender-child.html

Showalter, B. (2019, March 19). *Parents of autistic child threatened with removal of custody after rejecting puberty blockers*. Retrieved from Christian Post: https://www.christianpost.com/news/parents-of-autistic-child-threatened-with-removal-of-custody-after-rejecting-puberty-blockers.html

Sin Of Pride. (2019). Retrieved from All About God: https://www.allaboutgod.com/sin-of-pride.htm

Squires, J. (2015, July 29). *Pride is Your Greatest Problem*. Retrieved from Desiring God: http://www.desiringgod.org/articles/ pride-is-your-greatest-problem/

Stallard, M. L. (2019, January 03). *What Does the Bible Say about Work?* Retrieved from Bible Study Tools: https://www.biblestudytools.com/ bible-study/topical-studies/what-does-the-bible-say-about-work.html

Steele, J. (2019, February 26). *United Methodists Vote to Keep Traditonal Marriage Stance*. Retrieved from Christianity Today: https://www. christianitytoday.com/news/2019/february/united-methodist-lgbt-vote-conference-plan.html

Stetzer, E. (2016, September 12). *The State of the Church in America: When Numbers Point to a New Reality*. Retrieved from The Exchange: https://www.christianitytoday.com/edstetzer/2016/september/state-of-american-church-when-numbers-point-to-new-reality.html

Stewardship (theology). (n.d.). Retrieved from Wikipedia.org: https:// en.wikipedia.org/wiki/Stewardship_(theology)

Stonestreet, J. (2018, January 11). *Challenges Facing the Church in 2018*. Retrieved from Breakpoint: http://www.breakpoint.org/2018/01/ challenges-facing-church-2018/

Strand, P. (2018, April 01). *Incredible Proof for Why You Should Have Faith in the Bible*. Retrieved from CBN News: http://www1.cbn.com/cbnnews/us/2016/march/ incredible-proof-for-why-you-should-have-faith-in-the-bible

Sullivan, A. (2018, December 07). *America's New Religion*. Retrieved from Intellegencer: http://nymag.com/intelligencer/2018/12/andrew-sullivan-americas-new-religions.html

The Gospel of the Family. (2014, Septermber 30). Retrieved from Today's Catholic: https://todayscatholic.org/the-gospel-of-the-family/

Thomas A. Tarrants. (2011). *Pride and Humility*. Retrieved from Knowing & Doing, C. S. Lewis Institute: http://www.cslewisinstitute.org/Pride_and_Humility_SinglePage

Thomas, M. M. (1995, December 14). *The Church's Mission and Post-Modern Humanism*. Retrieved from Religion Online: https://www.religion-online.org/book-chapter/chapter-8-gospel-and-secular-culture/

Turek, F. (2018, July 19). *What Does Scripture Actually Say About Our Borders?* . Retrieved from Charisma News: https://www.charismanews.com/politics/opinion/72205-what-does-scripture-actually-say-about-our-borders

Velson, J. (2017, December 17). *Is The Planet Really In Danger Of Running Out Of Resources?* Retrieved from Forbes: https://www.forbes.com/sites/quora/2017/12/29/is-the-planet-really-in-danger-of-running-out-of-resources/#101218fc188d

Vox, L. (2017, June 02). *Why don't Christian conservatives worry about climate change? God.* Retrieved from The Washington Post: https://www.washingtonpost.com/posteverything/wp/2017/06/02/why-dont-christian-conservatives-worry-about-climate-change-god/?utm_term=.6194b653d2ab

Vryhof, B. D. (2017, January 01). *The Power of the Name of Jesus – Br. David Vryhof*. Retrieved from Society of Saint John the Evangelist: https://www.ssje.org/2017/01/01/the-power-of-the-name-of-jesus-br-david-vryhof/

Vyse, G. (2017). *Nancy Pelosi thinks Trump's presidency might be a message from God.* Retrieved from The New Republic: https://newrepublic.com/minutes/140984/nancy-pelosi-thinks-trumps-presidency-might-message-god

Wade, R. (2007, September 07). *Life in a Secular Culture – Christian Worldview Living in a Secular World.* Retrieved from Probe for Answers: https://probe.org/life-in-a-secular-culture/

Walsh, M. (2019, March 19). *WALSH: The Left Must Keep Its Bizarre Religious Doctrines Out Of The Classroom.* Retrieved from the Daily Wire: https://www.dailywire.com/news/44839/walsh-indoctrination-matt-walsh

What does the Bible say about hypocrisy? (2019). Retrieved from Got Questions?: https://www.gotquestions.org/Bible-hypocrisy.html

What Is Intercessory Prayer? (2019). Retrieved from CNB.com: http://www1.cbn.com/questions/what-is-intercessory-prayer

What is righteousness? (2019). Retrieved from Got Questions: https://www.gotquestions.org/righteousness.html

What is Social Justice? (2019). Retrieved from Pachamama Alliance: https://www.pachamama.org/social-justice/what-is-social-justice

What the Bible says about "Human Rights" and "Social Justice". (2019). Retrieved from The Bible Project: https://www.thebibleproject.com/explore/justice/

What the Bible Says About Family. (2019). Retrieved from Focus on the Family: https://www.focusonthefamily.com/family-q-and-a/faith/what-the-bible-says-about-family

Whelchel, H. (2018, April 10). *Do You Know the Purpose for Your Gifts and Talents?* Retrieved from Institute of Faith, Work & Economics: https://tifwe.org/the-purpose-gifts-and-talents/

World Population. (n.d.). Retrieved from Wikipedia.org: https://en.wikipedia.org/wiki/World_population#Ancient_and_Post-classical_history

Young, B. (2019). *Only Christians Understand True Justice.* Retrieved from Desiring God: http://www.desiringgod.org/articles/only-christians-understand-true-social-justice

www.ingramcontent.com/pod-product-compliance
Lightning Source LLC
Chambersburg PA
CBHW061757250726
48657CB00001B/172